A NARRATIVE OF EVENTS WHICH OCCURRED IN Baltimore Town DURING THE Revolutionary War

TO WHICH ARE APPENDED, VARIOUS DOCUMENTS AND LETTERS, THE GREATER PART OF WHICH HAVE NEVER BEEN HERETOFORE PUBLISHED

Robert Purviance

HERITAGE BOOKS
2023

HERITAGE BOOKS

AN IMPRINT OF HERITAGE BOOKS, INC.

Books, CDs, and more—Worldwide

For our listing of thousands of titles see our website
at
www.HeritageBooks.com

A Facsimile Reprint
Published 2023 by
HERITAGE BOOKS, INC.
Publishing Division
5810 Ruatan Street
Berwyn Heights, MD 20740

Originally published:
Baltimore, Maryland
Printed by Joseph Robinson
1849

— Publisher's Notice —
In reprints such as this, it is often not possible to remove blemishes from the original. We feel the contents of this book warrant its reissue despite these blemishes and hope you will agree and read it with pleasure.

International Standard Book Number
Paperbound: 978-0-7884-5132-4

PREFACE.

The following narrative was read before the Historical Society of Maryland, at their sitting in January, 1847. It has been compiled principally from documents which had been in the possession of my father, the late Robert Purviance, from the date of the events to which they refer. His family knew nothing of their existence until two years ago, when in a general search for papers in the custom house, they were found amid a vast collection of old documents, which had been the accumulation of more than half of a century. As they treated of events which had occurred in Baltimore during the Revolutionary war, of which few memorials had been preserved, I thought I would collect from them such as might be considered worthy of preserving, and present them, which I now do, in a publication, to the community, of whose early patriotism they bear so honorable a testimonial.

ROBERT PURVIANCE.

Baltimore, *January 15th,* 1849.

A NARRATIVE OF EVENTS, &c.

CHAPTER I.

Mr. Hume has remarked that "the curiosity entertained by all civilized nations, of enquiring into the exploits and adventures of their ancestors, commonly excites a regret that the history of remote ages should always be so much involved in obscurity, uncertainty and contradiction." In the indulgence of this natural curiosity, the American people have no regrets to experience, that their history is involved in obscurity, uncertainty and contradiction. The records which have been preserved of the planting of the different colonies, which were afterwards united as a great whole, and are now known as the United States, bear testimony to the pure and upright sentiments which directed the colonists in the building up of these great communities. Whether right or wrong in the crown of England undertaking to appropriate to itself the great wastes of a large portion of the North American continent, and allotting to such persons as might solicit of it, such of the vacant lands as they might require, is not now a question; for the principle seems to have been established from the earliest ages of civilization, that terri-

2

tories, either inhabited by savages, or destitute of any kind of population, belonged of right to the first discoverer; and that if he followed up his discovery by an actual occupation, his claim was good to it against all the world. That this principle, which has contributed to the civilization of the world, cannot be vindicated on the ground of natural right, will be admitted, when we reflect on the manner in which the great Creator has permitted the human race to be scattered over the earth. When man came from the hand of his Maker, he was endowed with all the powers requisite to fit him for the purpose for which he was created. To him was given dominion over the fowls of the air, and the fish of the sea:—"to subdue the earth," to "increase and multiply." As the race of man increased, it became necessary for them to extend the dominion they had at first occupied, in order to satisfy their increasing wants. A larger portion of the earth became necessarily occupied, and with the steadiness of the advancing wave, this increase of dominion continued. In the course of time, the tide of emigration reached the shores of Western America, and this vast continent became the dwelling-place of the descendants of those who began this emigration. Man seems early to have lost the knowledge of his Creator, but the impression that he is the creature of a superior power, has never been completely eradicated from his mind. If he had forgotten that the power to subdue the earth was an attribute which emanated from God, he has always felt that he had such a power, and he has not failed to exercise it. When this continent was first discovered, such a race of men as we have spoken of, were found to be in possession of it. As society advanced in civilization, to preserve such an intercourse between its parts, as would promote the great purposes for which it was created, it became necessary to establish such principles as would best secure this end. These principles, as established by the consent of the civilized portion of mankind, are what are now known by the familiar name of the laws of nations. They suppose a general civilization among nations, and provide for the intercourse of each with the other, upon principles adapted to such a state. Where, however, a people exist who are not yet formed into nations, but are still of so wandering a character, that the principles which bind those who are civilized, do not govern them in their intercourse with each other, they treat these wandering people in their intercourse with them, as mere tenants at will of the soil they occupy, and assume a right of dispossessing them, whenever they think the cause of civilization demands that its advocates should possess the nomadic land. After the discovery of America by Columbus, many of the nations of Europe became awakened by the success of his daring enterprise, and they, in their turn, fitted out ships to traverse the unfrequented seas, under the hope, that new discoveries would give to them, also, a rich harvest of glory. These new expeditions resulted in a discovery of the whole continent of North and South America, ; of a passage to India, and all Eastern Asia, by the Cape of Good Hope. These discoveries opened to Europe the fairest field of enterprise which had ever invited the industry and the skill of man. Heretofore, Europe, in the pursuit of maritime commerce, had been confined to the seas which wash her shores on the Atlantic and the Mediterranean. Her commerce with India was by land and the Mediterranean sea; and the expense with which such a trade would be necessarily burthened, would greatly diminish the benefits which otherwise must have attended its prosecution. After the discovery of the Eastern parts of America, England commenced her settlements in various parts of that portion of the continent. The charters granted to different persons for the purpose of making these settlements, were as various in the rights bestowed, as the views of the different applicants who succeeded in obtaining them. The colony which was planted in Massachusetts sprung from the persecutions experienced in England by the puritans, a class of people who had been distinguished by their opposition to the religious principles of the government. They sought an asylum where they thought they would be enabled to worship their Creator according to the dictates of their conscience, and not in conformity to the prescribed rules of the monarch. That asylum they found on Plymouth rock, and from this small spot of the earth, arose the colony of Massachusetts, the great leader in the war of our revolution. In the course of time, other colonies were planted, so that in the great war of 1754, which England waged against France, they numbered thirteen; and having obtained a population so numerous as to give them a mighty weight in the scale of power, they were called upon by the mother country to aid in destroying the power of France on this continent. That aid was furnished, and the history of their exertions reveals the illustrious fact, that to these, Great

Britain was mainly indebted for her exclusive dominion of all the territory which France had hitherto occupied. One would have thought, that the recollection of such services could never be obliterated from the mind of any recipient of the favor, be that recipient either an Empire, or an individual sovereign. The colony of Maryland, which had been planted by Lord Baltimore, in virtue of a grant made to him by Charles the First, had, at the time when this French war broke out, so far advanced in prosperity, that her population had reached to one hundred and fifty thousand persons, and her trade, with such parts of the world as her dependent character allowed her to have, was very extensive. And it is remarkable, that, so completely had the crown deprived itself of the power of taxation over the colony, that "it was covenanted on the part of the king, that neither he nor his successors should ever impose customs, taxes, quotas, or contributions whatsoever upon the people, their property, or their merchantable commodities laden within the province." In the war which began in 1754, Maryland does not appear to have heartily entered. She seems to have paid but little attention to the requirements of the crown, so far as they embraced supplies of men and money. Shielding herself, probably, under the broad prohibition which denied to the crown the right of imposing taxes, customs, quotas, &c., she thought she would consult her own convenience, as to the interest she ought to feel in carrying on a war for the aggrandizement of the crown itself. After the capture of Col. Washington, at the little meadows, the frontier settlements of Virginia and Maryland became endangered by the progress of the French arms. Maryland saw, in the disasters which had befallen those who had preceded her in their efforts to stay the French power, that her own situation was becoming critical, and with an energy, which in times of trial, she has been accustomed to exert, now entered into the contest. Her exertions were unabated until the capture of Fort du Quesne by Gen. Forbes, which put an end to the French power on the Ohio. From this period until the conclusion of the war, she does not appear to have taken any particular part in it. On the subject of taxation, to which it would be necessary to resort to give effectual aid, differences arose between the two houses of the legislature, and not being able to compose them by the ordinary methods of concession, they existed until the peace of 1763, when they naturally ceased.

This peace had scarcely dawned before the parliament of Great Britain had conceived the idea, that the burthens of the war ought not to be confined to those who reaped all its benefits, but that those who had given their blood and treasure, as aids, and who had no voice in saying, either that war was necessary at the time it occurred, or that a time for peace had now come, must divide them with her. The first intimation given by her that this participation of burthens would be required at the hands of her colonies, was in her celebrated stamp tax act. In Maryland, this act met with a resistance as bold and determined, as in any other colony of America. Among those of her sons who distinguished themselves in resisting this great encroachment, as well on the natural, as the colonial rights of the province, was Daniel Dulaney, Esq., a gentleman well known in the early history of Baltimore. In a pamphlet entitled, "Considerations on the propriety of imposing taxes in the British colonies, for the purpose of raising a revenue, by act of Parliament," with a force of reasoning that defied ingenuity to discover the slightest fallacy, he sustained the cause of America. This pamphlet of Mr. Dulaney was as much admired in England, by those who had resisted the enactment of the law in its passage through the British Parliament, as it was by those in this country who felt its irresistible power. It was indeed a subject of sincere regret to those who were accustomed to admire Mr. Dulaney in the zenith of his glory, that any circumstance should have subsequently occurred, to have prevented him from uniting with his friends, in all the questions which were connected with the differences with England. On the great one, the declaration of Independence, the aid of Mr. Dulaney was not given. The stamp act, in consequence of this determined opposition by the colonies, was repealed in the year 1766, but was followed by other obnoxious enactments, which appear to have been adopted, as much to try the experiment of taxation among an unwilling people, as from any desire to raise a revenue. The people determined that they would not permit themselves to be made the subjects of such galvanic experiments, and with a voice, that even the roaring of the mighty waters which separate England from America, could not drown, they proclaimed to England, that no British taxation should find a resting place in the colonies.

To such a height did these vexatious enactments reach, that in the year 1768, an association was formed in

Boston, by the merchants and traders of that town, for the purpose of opposing them by such restrictive measures as could not but be felt by the manufacturing interest of England, and through it, by the Government. In the month of August of that year, a letter was addressed by the merchants and traders of Boston to Messrs. Samuel and Robert Purviance of Baltimore, stating that they had been "sènsibly affected with the late acts of Parliament, imposing duties on sundry articles of commerce, with the express view of raising a revenue out of America, and with the embarrassments and restrictions the trade at present labors under, are fully convinced of the necessity of exerting themselves without any further delay, in a firm but peaceable manner of obtaining relief." In conformity to the determination thus expressed, they adopted several resolutions, all looking to the suspension of the greater part of trade, for one year, say from Jan. 1, 1769, to 1 Jan. 1770, which they had been accustomed to have with Great Britain. Certain articles, however, were excluded from the operation of these resolutions, in consequence of the necessity of their use, and their inability at that time to supply them from their own resources. They invite a co-operation with them on the part of the merchants of Baltimore, "especially when they consider, that upon their concurrence, their speedy concurrence, greatly depends the success of the measures entered into by the merchants of Boston." This letter was signed by Thomas Cushing, John Hancock, John Rowe, John Erving, Jr., Edward Payne, Wm. Phillips, and John Barrett; many of the names of which have subsequently brightened the pages of their country's history. I regret that I have failed in my researches of the many valuable documents of which I am in possession, to find among them the notice to which it was so eminently entitled, and which doubtless it received, as well from those to whom it was immediately addressed, as from those to whose confiding patriotism it appealed. I regret it the more, for the letter itself was the first communication ever made by the people of Boston, to the people of Baltimore, on the subject of the grievances to which they were primarily subject by the tyranny of British legislation. At this time, there was no paper published in Baltimore, and for any important communication, coming from any of the colonies, which was to be made public, the vehicle of Green's Maryland Gazette at Annapolis, or the Pennsylvania Gazette at Philadelphia, was made use of. In looking over the latter of these for the year 1770, I find, there was an account published of a town meeting held in Baltimore, in the month of June of that year, complaining of the inhabitants of Newport in Rhode Island, having violated "the non-importation agreement," which agreement, as appears from the proceedings of another meeting, held in October, 1770, had been entered into by the people of Baltimore in May 1769, according to the resolutions of Boston, as noticed above. As far as I can learn from these published town meetings, the people of Baltimore entered into the agreement, and for more than one year, with good faith, complied with all the requirements of the resolutions. But they found that other towns which had given the same pledge as they had, had so far departed from it, that a further observance of it on their part, while it but little benefitted the common cause, was working most injuriously upon them. Philadelphia, it appears, as well as Newport, had given cause of dissatisfaction to Baltimore, and of course, from her proximity to Baltimore, any trade she carried on, and which was denied to Baltimore, could not but be injurious to the latter. She therefore signified, in a town meeting held on the 24th Oct. 1770, "*that they were determined to depart from the non*-importation agreement, and import every kind of goods from Great Britain, such only excepted on which duties are, or hereafter may be imposed by the Parliament of Great Britain." A meeting was held at Annapolis on this subject, the 25th Oct. 1770, by some of the counties of other parts of the State, to which were deputed, by the Baltimore people, a committee to explain to them what were their new views and intentions, in consequence of the failure of other towns to adhere to their engagements. The delegates at this meeting, not feeling the inconveniencies to which Baltimore was subject by these defalcations, entered into resolutions to adhere to the original agreement, and denounced, not in the most courteous terms, "the merchants and traders of Baltimore," for endeavoring "to destroy that union and good faith so necessary at this, and at all *times*, for the safety and constitutional rights of these colonies." These denunciations were replied to in a well written article, published in the Pennsylvania Gazette. The writer shews, that those who opposed them, had but very little interest in the trade which they seemed desirous should wither under the blighting influence of defalcation; and at the same time he shews, what would be the steady adherence on the part of the "merchants and traders of Baltimore," if they could be assured of a faithful observance of the commom compact.

In consequence of the passage by the British Parliament of the Boston port bill,—a bill intended to shut out the people of Boston from a commercial intercourse with every part of the world,—the people of Boston assembled in town meeting at Fanueil Hall, on the 13th day of May, 1774, and voted, "that if the other colonies would come into a joint resolution to stop all importations from Great Britain, and every part of the West Indies, till the act blocking up the harbor be repealed, the same will prove the salvation of North America and her liberties." This resolve was transmitted to the people of Baltimore, in a letter written by Mr. Samuel Adams, to Mr. Wm. Lux of Baltimore. Mr. Adams, in his peculiarly energetic manner, said, "The people receive this edict with indignation. It is expected by their enemies, and feared by some of their friends, that this town singly will not be able to support the cause under so severe a trial. As the very being of every colony, considered as a free people, depends upon the event, a thought so dishonorable to our brethren cannot be entertained, as that this town will now be left to struggle alone." This resolve was not received direct from Boston until the 4th of June. A copy of it, however, had been sent by express to Baltimore, by the people of Philadelphia, and received here on the 23d of May. It was accompanied by an account of the action taken on it in Philadelphia. A meeting was called of "the freeholders and gentlemen of Baltimore county," on the 27th of May, by several gentlemen, who had met together on the reception of these papers from Philadelphia, for the purpose of calling the aforesaid meeting. These gentlemen were Robert Alexander, Robert Christie, Sen., Isaac Van Bibber, Thomas Harrison, John Boyd, Samuel Purviance, Jr., Andrew Buchanan, Wm. Buchanan, John Moale, Wm. Smith, Wm. Lux, John Smith. That meeting was held at the court house of Baltimore county, on Tuesday, May 31st, 1774. Capt. Charles Ridgely acted as chairman. There were eight resolutions adopted. The three first were dissented from by very inferior minorities; the remaining five were unanimously adopted. The first resolution expresses it as the duty of every colony in America, to unite in the most effectual means to obtain a repeal of the late act of Parliament for blocking up the harbor of Boston. Three dissentients.

The second concurred in the sentiment expressed by the Boston resolve, that if the colonies came into a joint resolution to stop importations from, and exports to Great Britain and the West Indies, the same would be the means of preserving North America and her liberties." Three dissentients.

The 3rd, the inhabitants of the county will join in an association to stop the intercourse at given days. Nine dissentients.

The 4th provides for the appointment of delegates to attend a general congress of deputies, from each county in the State, to be held at Annapolis, and delegates to attend a general congress from the other colonies. Unanimously assented to.

The 5th provides for breaking off all trade and dealing with that colony, province or town, which refuses to come into similar resolutions. Unanimously assented to.

The 6th appoints Capt. Charles Ridgely, Charles Ridgely, son of John, Walter Tolley, Jr., Thos. Cockey Dye, Wm. Lux, Robert Alexander, Samuel Purviance, Jr., John Moale, Andrew Buchanan, and George Risteau, as a committee to attend a general meeting at Annapolis, and that the same gentlemen, together with John Smith, Thos. Harrison, Wm. Buchanan, Benj. Nicholson, Thomas Sollers, Wm. Smith, James Gittings, Richard Moale, Jonathan Plowman and Wm. Spear, be a committee of correspondence, to receive and answer all letters, and on any emergency to call a general meeting, and that any six of the number have power to act. Unanimously assented to.

The 7th requires a publication of their proceedings to be made, "to evince to all the world the sense they entertain of the invasion of their constitutional rights and liberties." Unanimously assented to.

The 8th—a vote of thanks.

That all these resolves did not meet with the unanimity which was expected at the time, may be accounted for from this fact, that as some of them looked to a complete prohibition of all intercourse with Great Britain and her West India possessions, it was a ruinous interference with the most profitable branch of trade at that time carried on from Baltimore; and as the cause which had given rise to the suggestion of the prohibition, viz., the Boston port bill, being considered local in its character, it did not require such a sacrifice to be made to have it repealed. But the great majority took a more enlarged view of the subject. They viewed the bill as an encroachment upon American rights, and although in its immediate effects not reaching them, yet the day might come when the example of acquiescence in it, would be an encouragement to the British Parliament to enforce all the restrictions it then meditated imposing on the colonies. The majority reasoned correctly, and their constituents ratified their deed.

The gentlemen who had called the meeting of the 27th May, in consequence of the communication which had been received from Philadelphia on the 23d, considering the great importance of the subject of which it treated, felt that no time ought to be lost in making communications to other parts respecting it; for, from the many obstacles which prevented the rapid circulation of intelligence in those days, it would be a considerable time before they could hear any thing of these stirring events, unless a communication was hastened on from Baltimore. Accordingly, they addressed a letter to the people of Annapolis, and other parts of Maryland; Alexandria, Norfolk and Portsmouth, and Charleston. The general purport of these communications may be seen in the following letter to the people of Alexandria.

BALTIMORE, *25th May*, 1774.

GENTLEMEN,

On Tuesday last, we received by express from Philadelphia, a letter from the committee of correspondence at that place, enclosing a copy of the vote of the town of Boston; a letter from said town to the gentlemen of Philadelphia, advising their present unhappy situation, and requesting their brotherly advice on so interesting an occasion; copies of which vote and letter, the reply thereto, and the resolves entered into at Philadelphia, we now take the liberty of communicating to you, not doubting your readiness to take a friendly part in a matter so interesting to every American.

On receipt of these papers, we immediately convened the principal inhabitants of this place, in order to collect in some measure, their sense of the matter. The result was, that we appointed a committee, (of which you have the names annexed) to correspond with the committees of any neighboring colonies who may consult us on this or any other public occasion, and particularly, to promote a general correspondence of sentiments with our brethren through this province, in such measures as may, on mature consideration, be the most advisable to take on this alarming occasion. It has been proposed to convene the principal gentlemen of our country at large, in order to promote an application for calling the assembly of the province; but that we have postponed for the present, until we have the advice of our friends in Annapolis on the matter.

We hope and expect that the gentlemen of your province who distinguished themselves as the foremost in asserting the cause of American liberty, and opposing the scheme of parliamentary taxation, will now exert themselves with spirit and boldness in the cause of Boston, now violently attacked for defending the common cause of America; and we doubt not, that the gentlemen of your town in particular, will heartily concur in whatever measures may best serve the general good.

We are, with much respect,

Gentlemen,

Your most humble servants,

In behalf of the committee,

SAMUEL PURVIANCE, Jr.,

Chairman.

The committee of correspondence for Baltimore town:

Andrew Buchanan,	Wm. Lux,
Robert Alexander,	Thomas Harrison,
Wm. Smith,	Robert Christie, Sr.
John Smith,	Dr. John Boyd,
John Moale,	Isaac Van Bibber,
Wm. Buchanan,	Samuel Purviance, Jr.,

To the Gentlemen of Alexandria.

Immediately after the letter which was sent to Annapolis reached there, a meeting of the inhabitants was called in conformity to the desire expressed by the Baltimore committee; and the resolutions which they adopted, were in harmony with those which had emanated from Baltimore. An impression had got abroad that Baltimore was lukewarm in the cause, and it seemed to have thrown a gloom over the countenances of all; but when the resolutions which were adopted here were known, this gloom was dispelled, and confidence took the place of distrust. Mr. Alexander, one of the committee of correspondence, was the bearer of the resolutions to the people of Annapolis. In communicating to the committee the account of his reception at Annapolis, and the effect produced there by his mission, he says, "Baltimore town, considered in a commercial view, is with great justness, esteemed the place of most consequence in the province, and coinciding in sentiments with the metropolis, may have a happy effect on the whole." The gentlemen appointed as a committe for Annapolis were, Messrs. John Hall, Charles Carroll, Thomas Johnson, Jr., Wm. Paca, Matthias Hammond and Samuel Chase. They were "required to join with those who shall be appointed for Baltimore town and other parts of this province, to constitute one general committee; and that the gentlemen appointed for this city immediately correspond with Baltimore town, and other parts of this province, to effect such associations as will best secure American liberty." On the 26th May, this committee, in furtherance of the honorable commission with which they were entrusted, made the following communication.

ANNAPOLIS, *May 26th*, 1774.

To Messrs. Samuel Purviance, Jr., Wm. Buchanan, Andrew Buchanan, and the other gentlemen who compose the committee of correspondence in Baltimore town.

GENTLEMEN,

We feel the most sensible pleasure in the receipt of your letter, by the hands of Mr. Alexander. Nothing can be plainer than that the suffering of Boston is in the general cause of America, and that union and mutual confidence is the basis on which our common liberties can only be supported. We enclose you a copy of a letter wrote to Virginia, and of the resolutions past yesterday in our town meeting. It appears to us that much depends on the determinations of Virginia, which we shall

3*

nxiously expect. Unanimity in the Massachusetts, New York, Maryland, Virginia and South Carolina, which may reasonably be expected, bids fair for success. We cheerfully accept your invitation to a free intercourse, and shall most gladly harmonize with you in all possible measures, for the general good.

We are, gentlemen,

With the utmost sincerity and respect,

Your most obedient servants,

J. HALL,
CHARLES CARROLL,
THOMAS JOHNSON, Jr.,
Wm. PACA,
SAMUEL CHASE.

Mr. Hammond, absent.

In any struggle which Maryland might think proper to embark in opposition to the legislation of the British Parliament, it was all important for her that Virginia should be closely united with her in the opposition. Their geographical position in the colonies; their identity of interests from the common use of the Chesapeake Bay; and their kindred agriculture; all seemed to require that there should be an united action between them on the great question at that time pending. Virginia herself thought in this manner at that time, for on the very next day after this letter was dated, "the late members of the house of burgesses assembled at the Raleigh tavern in Williamsburg." The reason why this place and that manner was selected by the burgesses, for bringing their opinions before the people of Virginia, respecting the town of Boston, and the acts of the British Parliament, was, they had been deprived by the sudden interposition of the executive part of the government, from their giving their countrymen "the advice they wished to convey to them in a legislative capacity." They, however, were not to be intimidated by the arbitrary exercise of sovereign power. Their opinions had as much weight attached to them when uttered in a tavern, as if they had proceeded from the carpeted halls of legislation. The object of the meeting at the Raleigh tavern, was to form an association "in support of the constitutional liberties of America against the late oppressive act of the British Parliament, respecting the town of Boston, which, in the end, must affect all the colonies." A copy of this association, with a letter, dated the 31st May, 1774, from the committee of correspondence for Virginia, was sent to the committee of correspondence for Maryland at Annapolis, and by them transmitted to the committee of correspondence of Baltimore. The gentlemen who signed this communication were, Peyton Randolph, moderator; Robert C. Nicholas, Edmond Pendleton, Wm. Harwood, Richard Adams, Thomas Whitling, Henry Lee, Lemuel Riddick, Thomas Jefferson, Mann Page, Jr., Charles Carter (Lanc'r.) James Mercer, R. Wormley Carter, George Washington, Francis Lightfoot Lee, Thomas Nelson, Jr., Robert Rutherford, John Walker, James Wood, William Langhorne, Thomas Blackburn, Edward Berkely, Wm. Donelson, Paul Carrington, Lewis Burnwell, (Gloucester.)

The Baltimore committee received from the town of Alexandria, a letter, under date of the 29th May, 1774, in reply to theirs of the 25th. They remark "that following the good example you had shewn us, we called a meeting of the principal inhabitants of this town, who determined upon the choice of a committee for carrying on such correspondence as we judged necessary, for conveying our sentiments to the neighboring towns."

A letter was also received by the Baltimore committee, of the date of 2d June, 1774, in reply to theirs of the 25th May, enclosing resolutions which had been entered into by the people of Norfolk and Portsmouth. A committee of correspondence was formed by them, whose duty it was "to correspond with the several committees of the different commercial towns on the continent, upon the important subject of these papers, (those transmitted by the Baltimore committee) and acquaint them with the sentiments of the inhabitants of these towns, and to take such other steps for the relief of our suffering brethren of Boston, and the establishment of the rights of the colonies." The committee of Norfolk deemed the communication made to them by the Baltimore committee of so much importance, that they transmitted copies of it to the people of Charleston immediately, in a letter of the 31st May, which begins in the following noble strain: "The occasion is too serious to admit of apologies for this unsolicited communication of our sentiments to you, at this alarming crisis to American freedom; for the time is come, the unhappy era is arrived, when the closest union among ourselves, and the firmest confidence in each other, are our only securities for those rights, which as men, and free men, we derive from nature and the constitution."

On the 4th of June, 1774, the Baltimore committee transmitted to the Boston committee the resolutions which had been adopted, when the people of Baltimore were first made acquainted with the distresses of Boston. In the letter which conveyed these resolutions, they remark, "Could we remain a moment indifferent to your sufferings, the result of your noble and virtuous struggles in defence of American liberties, we should be unworthy to share in those blessings, which (under God) we owe, in great measure, to your perseverance and zeal, in support of our common rights, that they have not, ere now, been wrested from us by the rapacious hand of power." The committee of Boston, in reply to this communication, under date of the 18th of June, say, "We last evening received your affectionate letter of the 4th inst. enclosing your noble and spirited resolves. Nothing gives us a more animating confidence of the happy event of our present struggles, for the liberties of America, or affords us greater support under the distresses we now feel, than the assurances we receive from our brethren, of their readiness to join with us in any salutary measure, for preserving the rights of the colonies, and of their tender sympathy for us under our sufferings. We rejoice to find the respectable county of Baltimore so fully alarmed at the public danger, and so prudent and resolute in their measures, to secure the blessings of freedom to their country."

I have already observed, that the celebrated vote of the town of Boston, which took place on the 13th of May, 1774, together with a letter from the town of Boston of said date, was forwarded by express from Philadelphia to Baltimore, and received here on the 23d of May; and that immediate action was taken upon it by the people of Baltimore county. They addressed a letter on the 4th of June, to the committee of Philadelphia, responding in the most enthusiastic manner to the vote which had been transmitted to them, and from the language it makes use of respecting the propriety of holding a general congress of deputies from all the colonies, I infer, that the honor of first suggesting such an assembly to meet the great crisis which was then approaching, belongs as much to the people of Baltimore, as it has heretofore been considered, as in the exclusive possession of Virginia. Although the resolutions of Virginia which recommended it, was dated the 27th of May, yet the communication which announced it to the other colonies, was not dated until the 31st of May,—and on that day, the people of Baltimore, at their deferred meeting, made an equal recommendation of such a measure, and in conveying to the other colonies their sense of its propriety, they certainly speak as if they were the first to present this great measure for their approbation. They remark, in this celebrated letter, to the committee of Philadelphia,—" The idea we have formed of a general congress, as expressed in our fourth resolve, is by no means formed upon the opinion, or the necessity of such a congress, for the purpose of petitioning or remonstrating to the crown, or any branch of the legislature of Great Britain. The indignity offered by the ministry to every petition from America; the affected contempt with which they treated those transmitted in 1765, and every other since that time, leave us not the least ray of hope, that any application in that mode, would be productive of relief to the sufferings of Boston, whom we consider as a victim to ministerial vengeance, for wisely and justly opposing them in their arbitrary attacks upon American liberty. We have proposed the congress to settle and establish a general plan of conduct for such colonies that may think fit to send deputies. Their local circumstances and particular situation may render some little diversity necessary, especially should the same influence that has unhappily guided the councils of Great Britain continue to prevail."

A copy of these resolutions was transmitted also to the committee of Annapolis. The committee on receiving them, assented to the proposition they contained of calling a general congress, and immediately thereafter, addressed a communication to the committee of correspondence for Virginia on the subject of these resolutions. They say in their letter, "It is our most fervent wish and sanguine hope, that your colony has the same disposition and spirit, and that by a general congress, such a plan may be struck out, as may effectually accomplish the grand object in view." The committee of correspondence of Virginia reply to this suggestion of the Baltimore committee, on the 4th of August, in the following language. "The expediency and necessity, however, of a general congress of deputies from the different colonies was so obvious, that the meeting have already come to the resolutions respecting it." If there be merit in being among the first to suggest a great and leading measure, which from its peculiar fitness to produce the end contemplated by its creation, the recommendation of the general congress as suggested by the Baltimore committee, pre-eminently entitles them to its claim. That congress, according to these suggestions, did assemble, and from their deliberations resulted the declaration, that the thirteen colonies were free and independent states, and as such, were entitled to do all those acts, which of right, may be adopted by independent nations:—A congress, as described by Lord Chatham, "for solidity of reasoning, force of sagacity, and wisdom of conclusion, under such a complication of difficult circumstances, no nation or body of men can stand in preference to the general congress at Philahelphia."

The Baltimore committee appear to have lost no occasion to keep alive the spirit of patriotism, which had burned with intensity in their bosoms, from the moment they were made acquainted with the arbitrary legislation of Great Britain towards the town of Boston. Wherever their voice could reach, they were not backward in sending it forth; nor did they conceal their regrets, whenever any response was made by any of the colonies to their communications, which they thought fell short of their ardor. In a communication of the 17th of June, 1774, made to the committee of Norfolk and Portsmouth, they say, "Your letter of the 2d inst., which we received a few days ago, by General Lee, affords the highest satisfaction, in finding your sentiments on the Boston port bill, and other designs of administration, to correspond with our own, and the general sense of these important subjects. Having learned that there was a general meeting of the city and county of Philadelphia, to be held last Wednesday, we immediately despatched an express, with copies of your letters and resolves for that place and Boston, which would prove of singular service in obviating some unfavorable impressions made by the association of your late representatives, after the dissolution of your assembly, which were considered by many here (and we presume would by the people of Philadelphia) far short of that spirit and zeal by which the gentlemen of your colony have ever been distinguished.

The people of Chester, (Kent county,) had addressed the Boston committee on the subject of their grievances, on the 3d of June, in the kindest manner, and had proposed to open a subscription for the poor inhabitants of the town. The Baltimore committee, in a letter of the 13th of June, to the Boston committee, take notice of this generous offer in saying, "A proposal has been made by some gentlemen of Chestertown, in this colony, to open a subscription for the support of the poor inhabitants of your town, who may be most immediately distressed by the stagnation of business. Some of us have had the same object in contemplation, and determine to propose it to the general congress of deputies for the province, which, we doubt not, will be generally adopted." The committee of Boston, of which Samuel Adams was the chairman, in acknowledging this benevolence of Chester, say, "We cannot but applaud the spirit and determined virtue of the town of Chester in their public transactions. A happy concurrence of sentiment and exertion throughout the continent, at this interesting period, bodes well to the liberties of America. May this darling object forever attract our attention, and success crown the general struggle."

The Baltimore committee sent copies of their resolutions of the 31st May, to the counties of Anne Arundel and Frederick, immediately after their adoption. They were responded to by these counties within a few days after their receipt of them. The Anne Arundel committee, in transmitting their resolves, express a "fear that the Bostonians, whilst their brethren are deliberating, will lose all hope of an effectual union." Their resolutions breathe a spirit of American liberty, which it is delightful to contemplate. It was such a response to the Baltimore resolutions, that throughout the whole contest, no act upon their part ever falsified the pledges given on that day. The committee who were entrusted with the execution of these resolutions were, Thomas Beale Worthington, Charles Carroll (barrister,) John Hale, Wm. Paca, Samuel Chase, Thomas Johnson, Jr., Matthias Hammond, Thomas Sprigg, Samuel Chew, John Weems, Thomas Dorsey, Rezin Hammond, and John Hood, Jr. The committee for the town of Frederick, who were, John Hanson, Jr., Benjamin Dulaney, Thomas Schley, Conrad Grosh, Peter Hoffman, George Scott, Archibald Boyd, John Cary, and Christopher Edelen, acknowledging the receipt of the Baltimore resolves, say, "You will find, by ours, (which will be published in the next Maryland Gazette,) how far we agree with you in the mode proposed for obtaining a repeal of the late acts of parliament, as subversive of the liberties of America. It will always give us pleasure to receive any intelligence from you, relative to the redress of our grievances."

Having obtained the assent of Virginia, to the propriety of the meeting of a general congress, as suggested by the Baltimore committee, some difficulty arose as to the proper place of its meeting. The

Maryland committees appear to have been unanimous in the opinion, that Pennsylvania was the most proper place for this assemblage, and so represented it to Virginia. In a letter of the 26th of June, addressed "by the deputies for Maryland," to the committee of correspondence for Virginia, they say, "We are also directed to propose, that the general congress be held at the city of Philadelphia, the 20th of September next." "The limits of our province, and the number of its inhabitants, compared with yours, afford an opportunity of collecting our general sense, before the sentiments of your colony could be regularly ascertained, and therefore, as this province had the first opportunity, it has taken the liberty of making the first proposition." General, then Col. Washington, who was a member of the committee of correspondence, wrote on the 5th of August, to Mr. Thomas Johnson, Jr., of Annapolis, referring to this proposition, and said, "as the 1st of September or thereabouts, hath been fixed upon by all of them, (except your province) as a fit time, and as the time is now so near at hand as to render it difficult, if practicable, to change it without putting too much to the hazard; it was resolved here to abide by the general choice of Philadelphia, though judged an improper place, and to fix upon the 5th of September (as the South Carolinians have done,) for the time." This letter of Col. Washington, was transmitted by the committee of Annapolis to the Baltimore committee, accompanied with the proceedings of Virginia. They say, "The letter of Col. Washington to Mr. Johnson, you'll perceive, was not designed for public view. We are sorry that the meeting is so early as the 5th of September, but perhaps it will be better then, and at Philadelphia, than to run the risk of a new appointment." A communication was received at this time from the Norfolk committee, enclosing the Virginia resolves also. They remark, "that delegates appointed and instructed by almost every county in this extensive colony, met in convention with a great variety of different opinions, with respect to the mode of redress, altho' all agreed as to the oppressive and dangerous right claimed by parliament, of taxing and punishing us at their arbitrary pleasure."

I have thus detailed, with some minuteness, the events of 1774, so far as the documents which I possess, furnish the information. It will be perceived by these, that the only immediate agency which was required to be exerted by those to whom the appeal was made, on the enactment of the Boston port bill, was, to assemble the people together, and to know from them, in what light they viewed this most serious invasion of American rights; and to devise such a plan of united action, as would secure the colonies against future encroachments. This enactment, at this moment of time, was considered the most outrageous of the wrongs which had been inflicted. The stamp act had met with so decided a reprobation, that parliament was forced into a repeal of it within two years after its adoption. The enforcement of the tea tax was resisted by a resolution and courage that seemed almost to baffle the ingenuity of parliament, in devising schemes by which they could enforce an obedience to their laws. As the most effectual means to check the growing obstinacy of the colonies, it was thought, that the occlusion of the port of Boston would be an admonition that would be heeded by all. This state of things did call for, and was received by the whole people, with a determination not to submit to it. It will be seen by the resolutions adopted by the people of Baltimore, that the light in which they viewed this enactment, was, that "the colonies should come into a joint resolution to stop importations from, and exportations to, Great Britain and the West Indies, until the act for blocking up the harbor of Boston be repealed." This was a bold and decided recommendation, and when we take into the estimate of its character, the peculiar sacrifice it involved by an adherence to the resolution, it will be considered as among the most disinterested that patriotism ever adopted in behalf of a suffering country. Baltimore, at this time, although not having a population of more than five thousand people, carried on a most extensive commerce with such parts of the world as her colonial dependence permitted. Perhaps there was no part of America, which had such a proportionate trade as herself. The greater part of this must be sacrificed by the adoption of such a resolution;—yet this did not prevent its enactment, and among the leading men who were foremost in urging it to the favorable consideration of their countrymen, were her mercantile citizens.

As the preparatory proceedings for the great contest which was about to take place in the early part of the year 1775, and which had been directed by the committee of correspondence, were the result of the most exalted patriotism, it is a just tribute to the memories of the eminent gentlemen who composed that body, that they should not slumber in their graves unknown to those who are enjoying the rich inheritance of freedom they so largely contributed to transmit to them. Mr. Andrew Buchanan was a native of Baltimore county, and well known at the commencement of the disturbances, as General Buchanan, the Lieutenant of the county. He acted a conspicuous part as a member of the committee; and when any military services were required, General Buchanan was always present, with that portion of the militia he commanded, to render them. He died in the year 1786.

Mr. William Smith was born in Pennsylvania, and came to reside in Baltimore, about the year 1761. Mr. Smith was very early distinguished by an energetic, decided character. His intelligence soon attracted the notice of his fellow citizens, and as the active part he took in the committee confirmed all the previous impressions respecting him, he was transferred, soon after the organization of congress, to a seat in that illustrious body, where he served for three or four years. When the federal government went into operation, he was elected to congress, where he remained two years, and then voluntarily retired. He died in the year 1806.

Mr. John Smith, was a native of Ireland, but came to this country in childhood. His father settled in Cumberland county, Pennsylvania, where his son remained until 1759, when he came to Baltimore, where he resided until his death, in 1794. Mr. Smith was a gentleman possessed of strong, natural sense, and pre-eminently distinguished for the uprightness of his character. He was a member of the convention that formed the constitution of Maryland, and was afterwards a senator of the State. He was the father of General Samuel Smith, so long known and admired, as well for his military as his civil services; and of Mr. Robert Smith, who had been subsequently Secretary of the Navy, and Secretary of State.

Mr. John Moale was a native of Baltimore, and possessed a considerable landed estate when the revolution broke out. Urged by a love of country, which disdained to bargain for its value, he accepted the appointment of one of the committee, and remained honorably associated with them during its existence. He died in the year 1798.

Mr. William Buchanan, was by birth a Pennsylvanian, and emigrated to Baltimore about the year 1759. Mr. Buchanan manifested great zeal throughout the contest. He was appointed by congress commissary general of purchases, and continued in that capacity during the war. He died in 1805.

Mr. William Lux, was a native of Baltimore county, and when he accepted the honorable office which has given so much respect to those who were entrusted with it, he was a merchant. He was appointed vice chairman of this illustrious body, and in that capacity served for three years. He died in Baltimore, in May, 1778. Mr. Thomas Harrison, was by birth an Englishman. He had settled in Baltimore many years before the revolution, and had become possessed of a considerable landed estate in Baltimore town. Mr. Harrison continued as one of the committee during its ex-existence. He died in Baltimore, in the year 1782.

Mr. Robert Alexander and Mr. Robert Christie, Sr., were natives of Maryland. They took an active part in the operations of the committee, until the declaration of independence. This step caused their separation from their associates, and shortly after, both sent in their adhesion to the crown. They went to England, and there united with the loyalists in all the fortunes which awaited that class of Americans.

Dr. John Boyd, was by profession a physician. He was a gentleman of respectable talents, and of an amiableness of character that attracted general esteem. He often acted as secretary to the committee of which he was a member. He continued in the practice of medicine until his death, in the year 1790.

Mr. Isaac Van Bibber, was a gentleman of good sense and good education. He took an active part in defence of his country. Besides serving in the committee during its existence, there were other stations in which he served his country usefully. He lived a long time in Baltimore, but in the latter years of his life, he lived near Reisterstown, where he died in the year 1818.

Mr. Samuel Purviance, Jr., was a native of the county of Donegal in Ireland, and had emigrated to this country about the year 1754. He resided in Philadelphia until the year 1768, when he removed to Baltimore. He had, however, been united with his brother, Mr. Robert Purviance, in a commercial house, which had been established in Baltimore in the year 1763. Mr. Purviance was early distinguished by a bold and decided character. During his residence in Philadelphia, he had been among the foremost in opposition to the stamp tax, and from his familiarity with all the movements of Great Britain to fasten an odious system of taxation upon the colonies, he was selected by his colleagues, as the chairman of their body. In this capacity he remained during the existence of the committee ; and it will be seen in the present narrative, that this conspicuous station was sustained by him with a dignity, a talent and patriotism, that elicited the warmest approbation of some of the most distinguished of congress. Mr. Purviance was the writer of the greater part of the correspondence which emanated from the committee, of which he was chairman. His fate was an untimely one. In the year 1788, he was descending the Ohio, in company with several others, when the boat, on board of which he was, was captured by a band of Indians : some of the party made their escape. It was his misfortnne to have been secured by his captors, and led by them into the interior of their vast wilderness. From this moment, to him, his country, his family and friends, were lost forever. General Harmar, who at that time commanded one of the outposts of the frontier, had the country searched for him for more than five hundred miles, but in vain.

The committee of correspondence, elected on the 12th of November, 1774, were, Samuel Purviance, Jr., Robert Alexander, Andrew Buchanan, Dr. John Boyd, John Moale, Jeremiah Townley Chase, Wm. Buchanan, and William Lux.

The revolution may be said to have been begun, from the moment it was announced that the port of Boston was to be shut against all intercourse with the world. The colonies became inflamed at this renewed aggression on American rights, and determined, as we have seen by the proceedings of such of them as were in correspondence with the Baltimore committee, to meet it with all the vigor and energy which a just regard to their rights would naturally inspire. In the adoption of such measures as were best adapted to promote this end, the committees of correspondence throughout the country, appear to have been the chosen instruments of their fellow citizens, for seeing to their faithful execution. In Baltimore, it very early became a part of their duty, to have a surveillance over the conduct of all persons coming among them as strangers, and for this purpose, it was ordered by the committee, in December, 1774, "that Messrs. Richard Moale, Wm. Spear, Isaac Van Bibber, and Isaac Griest, do carefully observe the arrival of all vessels into the port of Baltimore, and immediately give notice of the same to the chairman." Ordered, "that public notice, by advertisement, be given to all masters and pilots, arriving at the port of Baltimore, that it is expected they will give information of such arrival, at their first landing, to some one of the said gentlemen." That many inconveniencies might result to strangers coming to a country, or town, which they had been accustomed to consider as a place to which resort might be had, whenever inclination should suggest the necessity or propriety of it, without being subject to a personal examination, we can readily conceive; but the indiscriminate admission of strangers into a community, struggling for the maintenance of rights, to secure which, an unanimity of opinion was a necessary element, would be an unwise act. In this point of view, therefore, the instituting of inquiries into the character of those who came to intermingle with them, will not appear to have been a harsh measure.

To this day, it is a practice in many of the countries of Europe, to require that all strangers, on arriving in any of their towns or villages, should make a report of themselves, and receive from the municipal authorities permission to stay, or an order to depart. In our towns, these inspections were confined to our revolutionary state; when that had passed away, all these restrictions ceased, and ingress and egress became as free as the air in which all breathed. These inspections appear to have been rigidly observed by the committee, and many persons, during their continuance, were either ordered away, or required to give security for the integrity of their conduct, whilst remaining. Shortly after the adoption of this resolution, information was given to the committee of observation, that the Rev. Mr. Edmondson had publicly asserted, "that all persons who mustered were guilty of treason; and that such of them as had taken the oath of allegiance, and took up arms, were guilty of perjury"—"and that the said William Edmondson had approved publicly of the Quebec bill." The committee were of opinion, "that such declarations have a tendency to defeat the measures recommended for the preservation of America and her liberties, and that it is their duty to take notice of persons guilty of such offences." Mr. Edmondson appeared before them as required, and made such an explanation of what he did say, with an apology for any part of it which might be considered offensive, that the committee accepted it and dismissed him.

To the committee of the first of May, 1775, information was given that a Capt. Richard Button "had used his influence to prevent people from mustering." Capt. Button was required to appear before the committee, to answer for this offence. The committee confined their sentence to the expression of the opinion, "that such conduct had a tendency to sow discord and division among us, as far as his contracted influence could extend, and highly injurious to the common cause of American liberty." Capt. Button acknowledged that he had done what he had been charged with, but said, "I promise and solemnly engage to this committee, that I will not, in future, make any attempts of this sort."

Mr. Griffith, in his annals of Baltimore, says, "that the people accused Mr. James Dalgleish, a foreign merchant, who had declared his aversion to the cause, and, therefore, as soon as he had been published as an enemy, he fled for safety." Mr. Dalgleish's case was this—he had been charged with saying, "that as soon as the English troops shall land here, he will join them against the Americans, it being a folly for him longer to deny his principles." "It was the opinion of the committee, that the said James Dalgleish, by his repeated offences, has discovered an incurable enmity to this country; and that it is dangerous to the cause in which we are all embarked, to encourage or countenance such a person among us. The committee think it therefore their duty, in conformity to the directions of the continental congress, to publish said Dalgleish, as an enemy to the liberty of Americans." Mr. Dalgleish tells his own story in the following note.

"Gentlemen,

I am just now come to town, and am told that my presence has been required before the respectable committee. I am sorry that my rash expressions (which till now, I knew nothing of) should have merited your inspection, or incurred your displeasure. I do not in the least deny, but that I made use of these unbecoming sentiments, being much intoxicated with liquor. I have, since the disagreeable difference between Great Britain and her colonies, been quite neuter with respect to either. Tho' to disapprove of the resolves of the continental congress, or the proceedings of the publick was quite foreign to my sentiments when sober. I am willing to waite on the gentlemen of the committee at their pleasure.

I am, respectable gentlemen,
Your humble servant,
JAMES DALGLEISH."

Mr. Dalgleish, apprehending that this denunciation of the committee might lead to some popular violence, withdrew from the town, and was never afterwards heard of.

A letter from Mr. James Christie, Jr., a merchant of Baltimore, directed to Lieut. Col. Gabriel Christie, of his Britannic Majesty's 60th regiment at Antigua, dated 22d of February, 1775, had been intercepted and laid before the committee. The letter says, "We are in such terrible confusion here with our politics, there is no depending on any thing, and that, added to other things, makes me wish myself out of the province. We are little behind the New Englanders, mustering, purchasing arms, ammunition, &c. We have some violent fanatical spirits among us, who do every thing in their power to run things to the utmost extremity, and they are gone so far, that we moderate people are under a necessity of uniting for our own defence, after being threatened with expulsion, loss of life, &c., for not acceding to what we deem treason and rebellion. The provost and family are very well, our public affairs vex him, and he wishes himself away, but I know not when, or if ever, that will happen. A part of yours, or any other regiment, I believe would keep us very quiet." Mr. Christie was arrested by order of the committee, and required to appear before them. He expressed his sorrow for the letter he had written; that he did not mean any harm by it, and that he was very willing to acquiesce in the determination of the committee. The committee unanimously decided, "that by representing in said letter, the people of this town to be concerned in treasonable and rebellious practices, and that a number of soldiers would keep them quiet, he, (Mr. Christie) has manifested a spirit and principle altogether inimical to the rights, privileges, and liberties of America: they do, therefore, think it their duty to advertise the said James Christie, Jr., as an enemy to this country, and all persons are desired to break off all connexion and intercourse with him." The committee further resolved, "that as the crime of which the said James Christie is guilty, is of so dangerous and atrocious a nature, they will lay the same before their delegates, at the continental congress, for their advice, and in the meantime it is ordered, that as Mr. Christie is confined to his bed, and cannot be removed with safety to a place of security, the same guard be continued at his house to prevent any escape, attempted either by himself, or the assistance of his friends." Mr. Christie had been engaged in mercantile business at Rock run, in Harford county, with Mr. John Wilson and Robert Christie, Jr. The day on which the committee gave in their decision on his conduct, these two gentlemen dissolved their partnership with him, determining not to be implicated with him in his adherence to the tory cause. Mr. Christie was kept under the surveillance of his guard, until the 24th of July, when he was discharged, upon giving an obligation, with five securities, not to depart the province without leave of the said committee, or the convention of Maryland. As a part of the resolution in his case was, to refer the question involved in it to the delegates to the general congress, Mr. Christie himself also referred his case to congress. That body referred him to the provincial convention of Maryland, to whom, in consequence of this reference, he presented a memorial on the 9th of August, 1775. Taking his own testimony, as furnished by the memorial, as conclusive against him as to the offence with which he had been charged by the Baltimore committee, the convention resolved, "that the said James Christie is, and ought to be considered as an enemy to America, and that no person trade, deal, or barter with him thereafter, unless for necessaries and provisions, or for the sale or purchase of any part of his real or personal estate, of which he may be at the time seized or possessed. Resolved, that the said James Christie be expelled and banished the province forever, and that he depart the province before the first day of September next."

To carry into execution the resolutions of the continental congress, respecting the public defence, it became necessary to raise in the province, the sum of ten thousand pounds, to be laid out in the purchase of arms and ammunition. The convention of Maryland, in assigning to each county the quota that would be requisite from it to make this amount, assigned to Baltimore county, as her proportion, £930. The Baltimore committee, to whom was entrusted the power of levying this amount on the inhabitants, affixed to the different districts of the county, the sums as follow :

District	£	s.	d.
Gunpowder Upper,	£79	17	6
North Hundred,	51	17	6
Middlesex,	33	7	6
Wyne Run,	53	00	0
Back River Upper,	112	00	0
Back River Lower,	39	5	0
Patapsco Upper,	50	10	0
Delaware Lower,	63	00	0
Middle River Upper,	43	10	0
Soldier's Delight.	87	12	6
Middle River Lower,	51	10	0
Patapsco Lower,	50	2	6
Pipe Creek,	34	5	0
Westminster,	51	00	0
Baltimore Town West,	72	7	6
Deptford,	30	2	6
Baltimore East,	26	12	6
	£930	00	0

I cannot forbear noticing the honorable solicitude felt by the committee, that their brethren of limited means should not be required to contribute any portion of the above taxation, for, in the resolution which levied it, they say, "care ought to be taken, to avoid laying any part of the burthen upon the people of narrow circumstances, hoping that those whom providence has blessed with better fortunes, will, by their generosity, supply the necessity of calling on those, whose fortunes are confined to the mere necessaries of life."

After the restrictive measures had been adopted, which confined the importations from Great Britain and the West Indies to particular commodities, it was apprehended that the article of salt was likely to become a subject of monopoly, and consequently, productive of great evil to the inhabitants. The committee took early steps to provide against such a state of things, but all their care did not effectually protect the people against the cupidity of the less patriotic. They were induced to repeat the admonition against monopoly, and to accompany it with a penalty more likely to secure a respect for it, than any heretofore suggested. "It was resolved in committee, November 13th, 1775: It appearing that the price of salt has been extended beyond the limits formerly fixed by this committee, and that much uneasiness has been thereby occasioned among the people; the committee are induced, therefore, to take the same into consideration, and after allowing a storage and loss of measure equal to so bulky and wasting a commodity, do recommend it to the venders not to sell the same above the rate of four shillings per bushel; and if any higher price has been hitherto given, the purchasers are desired to call on those from whom they bought for the overplus. If

5*

any sellers refuse to refund them, to complain to the committee; who do resolve that, if any sellers refuse to comply with the requisition, that they shall be immediately published as enemies to their country." It will be seen hereafter, that the supply of this article engaged very much the attention of congress; and the steps that were taken by the people of Baltimore, to aid them in their views. Various other resolutions were adopted by the committee this year, all looking as well to the well being of the community of whose interests they were the immediate agents, as to that of the country at large. Some of these, however, seemed to partake of sentiments adverse to republican liberty; but when we consider the state in which society was then placed by the dissolution of government, we may readily believe, that they were required by the then condition of the people, and were best calculated to promote to a successful issue, the cause which had given them birth. Society, in a state of revolution, is a different thing from society in a settled, organized state. In a state of revolution, a thousand things occur, to require to be met, not by the slow, deliberate caution which ought to mark the action of settled minds, but by the promptitude which applies the immediate remedy.

CHAPTER II.

On the 3d of July, 1776, the convention of Maryland resolved, "that a new convention be elected for the express purpose of forming a new government, by the authority of the people only, and enacting and ordering all things for the preservation, safety, and general weal of this colony." There was a provision made in the resolutions, for the new convention, for "two representatives for the town of Baltimore, in Baltimore county"—"but that the inhabitants of Baltimore town be not allowed to vote for representatives for Baltimore county;" "nor shall the resolution be understood to engage or secure such representation to Baltimore town, but temporarily, the same being, in the opinion of this convention, properly to be modified, or taken away, on a material alteration of the circumstances of that place, from either a depopulation, or a considerable decrease of the inhabitants thereof." Here we see the germ of that jealousy against Baltimore which took such a deep root in the state, and which has not yet been completely eradicated. Their anxiety respecting her representation was confined to the care of seeing, that this representation should be scrupulously confined to the number that she then reckoned as her population; and if a diminution of that took place, her representation was to be annulled. If an increase of numbers took place, no notice was to be taken of it; and for the space of nearly sixty years, she was confined to this original number, notwithstanding her population had reached one hundred thousand.

On the 6th of July, the convention declared, "that the king of Great Britain has violated his compact with this people, and that they owe no allegiance to him: we have, therefore, thought it just and necessary to empower our deputies in congress, to join with a majority of the united colonies, in declaring them free and independent states." The election for the town of Baltimore, in conformity to the resolve of the convention, was held on the 5th of August, and resulted in the choice of John Smith and Jeremiah T. Chase.

It appears to have been an important part of the duty of the committee of observation, to see that the military part of the defence of Baltimore was properly officered: that the companies were regularly filled up, and that they were to be in readiness to take the field when the occasion called for their services. They united in their appointments with others, and nominations when made by them, were generally confirmed by their associates in the appointing power. In the discharge of the duty of which I speak, the following instruction was given by the committee, in September, 1776. "The colonels of the militia having this day received an order from the convention, to nominate and appoint officers in this county for two additional companies of militia, to be immediately raised for the reinforcement of the continental army, which companies are to be enlisted until the first day of December next; each man is to be allowed a month's advance, and a bounty of £3, and their pay is to commence from the time of enrolment. And whereas, in many parts of this county, the battalions are not yet completed, nor the field officers appointed, Resolved, that the field officers of the battalions already formed, be desired to meet the committee on Friday next, at 10 o'clock, jointly to fix on the nomination of officers for the said two companies of militia, when such gentlemen as are desirous of commissions, are requested to apply, and that the respective battalions, and the companies of militia already formed, be desired to meet on Saturday next, when such as are inclined to enter as volunteers, will have an opportunity."

There was a part of the population, who, when they were required to subscribe to an association, which had been formed in the province, at the recommendation of the general congress, refused to do so. The object of this association was, for the general defence of the province, and those who refused to unite in such a design, were generally considered as inimical to American liberty. They were known by the name of non-associators, and as such, were subject to a fine of a given amount. Whether this was payable at stated periods, for a continued obstinacy, or that the sum first levied was considered a sufficient compensation for their neutrality, I have not been enabled to discover; but certainly the fines first levied were exacted with rigor. A person by the name of Robert Dow seemed to be so much under the influence of conscientious motives, that he could not reconcile it to himself to become a patriot, and for his refusal to enlist under the sacred banner of his country's cause, he was fined five pounds. This appeared to him to be a large sum to which his conscience had subjected him, and therefore plead earnestly, that "he had a wife and six children to maintain; that he is unable to pay the fine, and therefore requests the committee to mitigate it." The committee take this laconic notice of it. "In committee, 29th of July, 1776. Read and rejected."

Per order,

W. LUX, *Vice-Chairman.*

Another person, by the name of Abram Evening, was brought under the notice of the committee, for his singular opposition to American rights; and from the complexion of a communication from him on the subject of his grievances, we are naturally led to the conclusion, that the committee had an arduous task, in forcing men to defend their country's rights. "I intend," says Mr. Evening, in a letter to a friend, "since there is nothing to be done in your business worth speaking of, to send the books and papers into the country about thirty miles from Baltimore, that in case I cannot stay in such a violent place, they may be safe. You may be surprised at my writing in this style, but when you reflect of the disposition of the fanatics, you will approve of it. You must know it is against me to take up arms, or do any thing that attends to it against my native country. I am confident, from particular circumstances, that I shall mention, at a more convenient opportunity, that I cannot long remain in Baltimore, because I have got too many enemies; for instance, a few weeks ago, as I had nothing to do, I intended to go in the schooner to Cambridge, and two or three more places, to get the papers to send home; accordingly, the skipper waited on the chairman of the committee, to get a pass, but they would not give me one, except I would give security, under the penalty of £350 stg. for my return, and that I would not correspond with the king's officers; this was done; but after all, they would not give me the pass, except I would pay my £10 fine, for *not associating*, this I will not do till the last extremity." The continental congress having recommended that adventures be made for procuring arms and ammunition, and it being necessary that a particular committee be appointed to superintend the loading of vessels: Resolved, that Messrs. Samuel Purviance, John Smith, Wm. Buchanan, Benj. Griffith, Isaac Griest, Thomas Gist, Sr., and Darby Lux, be a committee for that purpose; and that they be on oath to keep their proceedings secret. The following resolve was adopted by the committee, in harmony with the above recommendation. Jan. 8th, 1776, Resolved, that no person shall, after the publication hereof, under any pretence or direction whatsoever, presume to load any vessel, or after being loaded, shall attempt to depart this port without proper permits from this committee, as they shall answer to the country.

DAVID McMECHEN, *Secretary.*

Another resolution respecting arms was adopted, Feb. 27th, 1776. "All persons in this county, possessed of any arms, belonging to the public, are hereby directed to deliver the same to the committee of observation, at Baltimore town, as speedily as possible; the council of safety having given them orders to collect and repair the same. It is to be hoped that the urgent necessity of an immediate compliance with this requisition, will induce every one who has any of said arms, to attend thereto without delay."

By order of the committee,

GEORGE LUX, *Secretary.*

In March, 1776, Capt. Squires, the commander of the British sloop of war Otter, who had been cruizing about in various parts of the bay, made a demonstration in the Patapsco river, with various boats, which produced a very great alarm in the town. Capt. Nicholson, the commander of the Defence, a ship belonging to the state of Maryland, was at that time in Baltimore. He soon got under weigh to drive these marauders from the river, which he did in a short time, and captured four or five of the boats. It was the occasion of this alarm that gave rise to the necessity of throwing up batteries on Fell's point; the fortifying of Whetstone point with eighteen guns; and the sinking of vessels at the fort. These defences were considered at the time as invaluable, and the aid which the militia of the surrounding country afforded, called for the grateful thanks of the people. From Harford county, a battalion marched to Baltimore, whose services it afterwards became unnecessary to accept. Col. Rumsey, to whose regiment the battalion belonged, in acknowledging the receipt of the communication, made to them by the Baltimore committee, expressive of their sense of the patriotism of the battalion, says, "That battalion, sir, esteem it but their duty to march to the assistance of any part of the province when attacked, or in danger of it. But they march with greater alacrity to your assistance, from the pleasing memory of former connexions, and a sense of the value and importance of Baltimore town, to the province in general." Nor was this devotion to Baltimore confined in the hour of her need, to the citizens of her own state. The borough of York wrote on the 10th of March to the committee: "Our committee resolved instantly to raise a good rifle company, to be ready to march on an hour's warning to your province, in case you should judge it necessary, and signify the same to our committee." This is not a solitary instance of this patriotic borough's offering her valuable aid to Baltimore. In the war of 1812, a company sent by her, united with the Baltimore troops, on the day of her celebrated battle with the British army near North point, and no troops on that day, were more entitled to the honors which their valor won, than those from York. The committee presented an address to Capt. Nicholson, acknowledging the valuable services he rendered to the town, by driving Capt. Squires away from the river. His answer to them is worthy of being transcribed here.

To the committee for Baltimore county.

GENTLEMEN,

I return you my most sincere thanks for your polite address. In support of the rights and liberties of my country, I cheerfully undertook the arduous task of my present office, and am exceedingly happy, in finding my conduct stand approved, by so respectable a body as the committee of Baltimore county. I am likewise to assure you that the officers, volunteers, and others on board the Defence, consider your address as doing them the highest honors.

I am gentlemen,

Your obedient, humble servant,

JAMES NICHOLSON.

In the beginning of April, 1776, Capt. James Barron, commanding one of the public vessels employed in the Chesapeake bay, for its defence, fell in with and captured a small vessel, which had been sent by Lord Dunmore, who was at that time on board of one of the British squadrons stationed in the bay, to Annapolis, for the purpose of transmitting certain letters from Lord George Germain, the British Secretary of State, to Governor Eden of Maryland. These letters were placed in the hands of Alexander Ross from Pittsburg, a person who had been well known as a violent British partizan. The letters were sent by Capt. Barron to General Lee, who at that time was in Williamsburg, and who, on a consultation with the committee of safety of that place, sent them to Mr. Samuel Purviance, the chairman of the committee of safety at Baltimore, accompanied with the following letter.

WILLIAMSBURG, *April* 6, 1776.

DEAR SIR,

As I know not to whom I can address this most important note, with so much propriety and assurance of success as yourself, this crisis will not admit of ceremony and procrastination; I shall, therefore, irregularly address you in the language, and with the spirit of one bold, determined free citizen to another; and conjure you, as you value the liberties and rights of the community of which you are a member, not to lose a moment, and in my name, if my name is of consequence enough, to direct the commanding officer of your troops at Annapolis, immediately to seize the person of Governor Eden: the sin and blame be on my head. I will answer for all to the congress. The justice and necessity of the measure will be best explained by the packet, transmitted to you by the committee of safety from this place. God Almighty give us wisdom and vigor in this hour of trial.

Dear Sir,

Yours, most affectionately,

CHARLES LEE.

To Samuel Purviance, Esq.,

Chairman of the Committee.

That the public should be made early acquainted with the contents of these letters, and that the person to whom they were addressed, should be dispossessed of all power to aid the British government in their views as set forth in these letters, Mr. Purviance, believing, from the peculiar circumstances attending this case of Governor Eden, that the powers he had been invested with, as the chairman of a committee, whose duty it had been from the commencement of the disturbances, to hold such a supervision, as well over the conduct of those who were the residents of the colony, as of those who might come among them, either as transient persons or traders,—would extend to such a case as the letter to General Lee directed his attention to, he instructed Capt. Samuel Smith of Col. Smallwood's battalion, on the 14th of April, to go to Annapolis, and seize the person and papers of Governor Eden, and detain him until the will of congress were known. The same day on which this order was given to Capt.

Smith, the Baltimore committee addressed the following letter to congress.

In Committee, Balt., 14*th of April*, 1776,
10 o'clock, P. M.

Hon'ble Sir,

The enclosed copies of letters were just now received by our committee, by express, from the council of safety of Virginia, with desire that they might be forwarded to you instantly. Indeed, they contain matter, we think, of too much importance to have been delayed a moment. In consequence whereof, we have prevailed on our commanding officer here to appoint Mr. David Plunkett, a Lieutenant, in whose prudence and industry we can rely, to wait on you with this; and if your honorable body should think it necessary to take any steps, or give any instruction to the council of safety on the occasion, he will wait your command.

We have the honor to be,
With the greatest respect,
Honorable Sir,
Your most obedient servants,

SAMUEL PURVIANCE, Jr., *Chairman.*
WILLIAM LUX, *Vice-Chairman.*
JAMES CALHOUN,
THOMAS HARRISON,
BENJAMIN NICHOLSON,
WILLIAM BUCHANAN,
JOHN SMITH,
JOHN BOYD,
JOHN STERETT.

The Hon. John Hancock, Esq.,
Prest. of the Congress, Philadelphia.

To which Mr. Hancock immediately replied.

PHILADELPHIA, *April* 16*th*, 1776.

GENTLEMEN,

I received, and immediately communicated to congress, your letter of the 14th, with the important papers enclosed. In consequence of which, the congress have resolved that the person and papers of Governor Eden be immediately seized by the committee of safety, to whom I write by this opportunity. The person mentioned in the enclosed resolution, (Mr. Alexander Ross) is represented as a dangerous partizan of administration, who has lately been with Lord Dunmore, and it is suggested on his way to the Indian country, to execute the execrable designs of our enemies. I have no doubt, but you will exert your utmost endeavors in seizing and securing him.

I am, with respect,

Gentlemen,

Your most obedient servant,

JOHN HANCOCK, *President.*

Honorable Committee of Baltimore.

P. S. You will please not to make public mention of the resolution respecting Governor Eden, until the committee of safety have executed it.

The council of safety at Annapolis, took offence at this order of Mr. Purviance, and interfered to prevent its execution. Their disapprobation of it, proceeded less from an objection to the measure itself, than from an implied disrespect of their own authority. The convention of Maryland, which sat in a short time afterwards, in consequence of a complaint laid before their body by the council of safety, relative to this conduct of Mr. Purviance, appointed a commitee to inquire into the steps necessary to be taken to make him amenable at their bar. This committee reported, first, "That the said Samuel Purviance, since the rising of the last convention, hath usurped a power to direct the operations of the military force of this province (at a time when the council of safety, to whom the same solely and properly belongs in the recess of convention, was sitting, and might, without inconvenience, have been applied to) as appears by his letter of instructions to Capt. Samuel Smith, of Col. Smallwood's battalion, bearing date the 14th day of April last, a copy of which, attested by the clerk of the council of safety, your committee refer to.

"Secondly, That the said Samuel Purviance, being at the time of writing the said letter, and giving the said instructions, chairman of the committee of Baltimore county, did write the said letter, and give the said instructions under color of his said office of chairman, and as if at the request of the said committee; whereas, the said committee were not consulted thereon, nor made acquainted therewith, as appears by the said letter and instructions, and by the proceedings of the said committee, attested copies whereof, among the said papers, are referred to.

"Thirdly, That the said Samuel Purviance, by writing and speaking, and particularly by a letter by him, written to the president of the congress, some time about the middle of April last, hath unjustly represented the convention and council of safety, as irresolute, and afraid to execute the trusts reposed in them, and endeavored to draw a suspicion upon them of a want of spirit and zeal in the execution of their duty."

In about two weeks after this report was made by the committee to the convention, that body came to the resolution of censuring Mr. Purviance for this conduct towards Governor Eden, concluding it in these terms: "In consideration of his active zeal in the common cause, and in expectation that he will hereafter conduct himself with more respect to the public bodies necessarily entrusted with power, mediately or immediately by the people of this province, and will be more attentive to propriety, this convention hath resolved, that the said Samuel Purviance, for his said conduct be censured and reprimanded, and that Mr. President do from the chair, censure and reprimand him accordingly, and that he thereupon be discharged.

"And thereupon, the said Samuel Purviance Jr., being called in, and being at the bar of this house, Mr. President communicated to him the resolve of convention, and did censure and reprimand him accordingly."

It will be observed by the third section of the report of the committee to the convention, that Mr. Purviance was charged with having "written a letter to the president of congress, some time about the middle of April last, hath unjustly represented the convention and council of safety, as irresolute and afraid to execute the trusts reposed in them." Mr. Purviance, on knowing that the committee of the convention had founded a charge of misconduct against him, upon their being made acquainted with the existence of this letter, wrote, on the 2d of May, to his friend Mr. Richard Henry

Lee, in congress, to know how the knowledge of this letter, escaped from their body, since it was intended to be confidential. Mr. Lee, in reply to him under date of the 6th of May, says: "Dear Sir, I received yesterday, your favor of the 2d inst, and in answer to that part of it desiring to know if Mr. Hancock gave a copy of your letter to any person, I must say, that I do not know whether or not, but I am inclined to think he has not. This business appears to me thus: When Mr. Hancock received the despatches from Baltimore, he proceeded to read the whole in congress, and among others, a letter containing observations on the council of safety of Maryland, relative to the timidity of their councils, which it appears he had not previously read in private, because when he came to that part of it which mentioned its being written in confidence he stopt, and observed it was private, and proposed it should be so considered, but as he had read so much of it, he went on, but read no name at the bottom, and in the debate consequent upon it, 'twas supposed to be anonymous, and it was conjecture alone that fixed you as the author. I should have certainly informed you of this if I had then found myself at liberty to do it, and when I heard from you of your summons before the council, it was too late for a letter to reach you before your appearance at that board. But the idea of drawing from the mouth of a person accused, his own condemnation, is reprobated by English jurisprudence, and is the practice only of inquisitorial or star chamber tyranny. I should incline to think that this prosecution will be carried no further; at least, I am sure the time is quickly coming, when violence from without, will render absolutely necessary a perfect union within." Mr. Purviance had written on the 23d of April, to Mr. Lee, on this same subject, to which Mr. Lee in reply, remarks: "The public of America is a generous public, and when appealed to, will readily distinguish things dictated by the general good, though irregularly executed, from such as are evil in their nature, and merely the suggestions of folly and wickedness. I am sure, a generous community will not suffer any person to be persecuted for the former, nor would I scruple in such a case, to say as of old, Provoco ad populum, and then look the proudest connexions in the face, trusting to the wisdom of the object, and the integrity of design, notwithstanding the manner might be something unusual."

On the second day after the convention of Maryland had reprimanded Mr. Purviance, they came to the following resolutions respecting Governor Eden.

"Resolved, that it is the opinion of this convention, that the council of safety of this province, upon the subject of the late intercepted letters to Governor Eden, duly and properly exercised the powers delegated to them.

"Resolved, that it is the opinion of this convention, that upon the evidence before them of the correspondence which his excellency, Governor Eden has, from time to time, held with administration, it does not appear that such correspondence has been with an unfriendly intent, or calculated to countenance any hostile neasures against America." After recapitulating in the ›reamble of the last resolution, the contents of these intercepted letters; and expressing how far the governor was bound, so long as he executed the powers of governor, to obey the instructions of the administration contained therein, they resolved, "that it be signified to the governor, that the public quiet and safety, in the judgment of this convention require, that he leave this province, and that he is at full liberty to depart peaceably with his effects." As the committee of safety of Virginia was that body which originated the design of arresting Governor Eden, Mr. Purviance deemed it proper that he should communicate to them the result of the agency respecting it which he had, in consequence of the intercepted correspondence having been transmitted to him. He says, in his letter to the committee, "We herewith transmit you copies of the resolves of the congress, respecting the seizing and securing Alexander Ross, and the letter of the President of the congress, informing us of their resolution, that the person and papers of Governor Eden be immediately seized, by our council of safety, to whom that resolution is transmitted. Instantly upon receiving your letter by express, we appointed three of our body to wait on the council of safety, to communicate the intelligence received, and to use their utmost endeavors to have Governor Eden put under arrest. Our council have thought it sufficient to take Governor Eden's parole of honor, not to depart the province till the meeting of the convention of Maryland." The convention of Virginia were very much dissatisfied with the convention of Maryland respecting the manner in which they had treated their recommendation of the immediate arrest of Governor Eden. On the 31st of May, they "Resolved unanimously, that the committee of safety be directed to write a letter to the president of the convention of Maryland, in answer to his letter of the 26th inst., expressing the deepest concern at the proceedings of that convention, respecting Governor Eden, and our reasons for not becoming accessory thereto, by giving him a passage through this colony, or the bay adjoining: that we would with reluctance, in any case, intermeddle in the affairs of a sister colony, but in this matter we are much interested." "That considering the intercepted letter from Lord George Germain to Governor Eden, in which his whole conduct, and confidential letters are approved, and he is directed to give facility and assistance to the operations of Lord Dunmore against Virginia, we are at a loss to account for (the council of safety of Maryland,) their having neglected to seize him, according to the recommendation of the general congress." From this view of this celebrated transaction it will appear, that Mr. Purviance, in anticipation, did that which congress required to be done, when the facts of the case came to their knowledge, and which it was natural to suppose they would do. He did that, which Virginia, more deeply interested in the question than any of the other colonies, said was proper to be done, and the preventing of its execution by the convention of Maryland, called forth her severest disapprobation. He was censured by his own province, but he bore her frown with the submission of a patriotic citizen, and with the dignity which a conscious sense of honor will always inspire.

An election was to have taken place on the 3d of July, for delegates to represent Baltimore county in the general assembly of the province, by virtue of a writ, directed from his excellency, Robert Eden, Esq., to the sheriff of the county. So completely had the minds of the people, at this time, been made up to shake off all dependence upon Great Britain, that they determined this writ should be the last testimonial of her past power, and that a disobedience of it should be the first signal of the existence of the power which was hereafter to govern the new born republic. The convention of Maryland ordered, on the 25th of June, that the said writ be not obeyed, and that no election be made in consequence thereof:—This order was obeyed, and the authority of England in Maryland, became extinct forever. Governor Eden was now permitted to leave the colony. The circumstances under which he embarked, were not as favorable to his character, as they would have been, had the convention have permitted the order of the Baltimore committee for his arrest, three months before, to have been executed. He embarked on board "his majesty's ship Fowey," the 24th of June, but his baggage was detained in consequence of the supposed attempt of Capt. Montague, the commander of the ship, to take off runaway slaves. In reply to a communication made to him by Mr. Carroll, the vice-president of the council of safety, he says, "I can only say that Capt. Montague's order to receive on board, and give protection to all British well affected subjects, are positive, and that he does not consider it in his power, consistently with these orders, to comply with your request."

On the 29th of July, the declaration of independence was read at the Court house. It was received with great acclamation; at night the town was illuminated, and at the same time the effigy of George the third was carted through the town, and committed to the flames.

In coming to this determination of independence at last, it appears to me, it was approached by the great body of the people of Maryland, with a cautious, trembling step. When the people met together in nearly all the counties of the province, to consult as to the measures that ought to be adopted after the passage of the Boston port bill, they looked to scarcely any other defensive weapon than restrictions upon their trade with Great Britain and her dependencies, believing they would be more efficacious in driving her from the mad policy she was pursuing towards the colonies, than any other measure they could adopt. They considered that her maritime trade was that which gave her the exalted rank she maintained among the nations of the earth, and in proportion as her colonies were instrumental in the reduction of that trade, in that proportion would be the diminution of her rank. Whatever weight may be ascribed to these opinions by those who indulged in them in many parts of the province, I think they had less weight in Baltimore county than elsewhere. Their resolutions looked to something more than mere restrictive measures on trade, and the suggestion which certainly first came from them in Maryland, of a general congress of all the colonies, appears to me to be an evidence of it. In the letter, of which we have already spoken, which was transmitted to Philadelphia, communicating the early resolves of the Baltimore people, the language was, "We have proposed the congress to settle and establish a general plan of conduct, for such colonies that may think fit to send deputies." It was very natural, however, for a people who owed their very existence to the nation they were now called upon to separate from, that before they should do that which would involve them in difficulties and distresses, from which long years might not relieve them, they would weigh well all the consequences: and in deciding at last, that *these* were not to be compared with the rich inheritance which had been transmitted to them by their fathers, who had planted the colonies, they offer to the world one of the sublimest spectacles which have ever been presented to mortal eye.

Mr. Robert Christie, Jr., who, as sheriff of the county, it had been supposed was the proper person to read the declaration of independence to the people at the Court house, refused to appear there for such a purpose. In consequence of this refusal on his part, threats had been made against him, which he deemed it prudent not to brave, and therefore he withdrew from the town. As these threats indicated a state of feeling in the public mind which the committee thought boded no good to the common cause, they promptly met them by such a conciliatory resolution as dispelled the threatened evil.

"Extract from the minutes of the committee of observation for Baltimore county, July 30, 1776. The chairman being informed by Mr. Robert Christie, Jr., the sheriff of this county, that he had reason to be apprehensive of violence being offered to him, the said sheriff, on account of his not attending to read the declaration of independence last Monday, agreeable to the desire of the committee, and that from those apprehensions, he would be under the disagreeable necessity of retiring to the country, and withdrawing himself from the public service,

"Wherefore, resolved, that this committee do declare their utter disapprobation of all threats or violence being offered to any persons whatever, as contrary to the resolves of congress, and the sense of the convention of this province: That they conceive themselves bound to protect (as far as in their power) the civil officers, in the discharge of their duty. That they do expect of, and call upon every good citizen and friend to his country, to assist them in their endeavors to preserve the peace and good order of society, and to prevent all riots and tumults, and personal abuse and violence to individuals. That the good people of Baltimore, having hitherto been so respectfully attentive to the resolves of this committee, on all occasions, they flatter themselves that due regard will be paid to this recommendation."

SAMUEL PURVIANCE, JR.,

Chairman.

CHAPTER III.

THE convention of Maryland met on the 14th of August, 1776, for the purpose of "establishing a bill of rights, and the formation of a new government, on the authority of the people only." These important measures were adopted by the convention, on the 8th of November following. For the introduction of the new government, an election was required to be held on the 25th of November, of the same year, for the electors of the senate, which body were afterwards to meet on the 9th of December, and then choose senators; and an election was to be held on the 18th of December, for delegates to serve in the general assembly. Committees of observation were required to be elected also, on the 25th of November. These committees were to be invested with the powers given by this and former conventions, and continue until the 10th of March, 1777, "or until the general assembly of the state should make further order therein."

This constitution of government was about one of the best political creations which resulted from the labors of those who were called upon, by the peculiar circumstances of the country, to provide new systems of government for the people. It gave an ample protection to the people for whose immediate benefit it was established: It became an able auxiliary in the great cause of American liberty, and so much has it commanded of the affections of the people, that in the seventy-two years of its existence, there have been fewer alterations in its organic character, than in any other of the states of the union during the same period.

In consequence of the approach of General Howe's army towards Philadelphia, General Putnam who commanded there, and General Washington, who at that time was in Philadelphia, recommended that congress should remove for the present to Baltimore; and, on the 20th of December, 1776, in conformity to these opinions, they removed hither, and commenced their session.

There was a great scarcity of flour, bread and iron in the eastern states, at the commencement of the year 1777. The military operations of the enemy, at this time, being pretty much confined to New Jersey, New York and Pennsylvania, the intercourse was very much interrupted by these. Congress looked towards Baltimore, as being more exempt from these obstructions, than any of the other large ports on the sea board, as the resource from which this supply was to come. They directed their eastern agents to send their orders here, and, in consequence, many, to a large extent, were received; and I believe, in every instance, the supply was obtained. Some time before this, Messrs. Samuel and Robert Purviance, had become the agents of congress, as well for obtaining all the supplies that might be required here, as in general for such financial operation, as the emergencies of congress might require in the south. This will account for the reason why many of the letters which are now published,

7*

were directed to them, either as partners or individuals. This agency was continued during the whole period of the war; and the vast expenditures which were made, could the accounts of them all, meet the public eye, would present the difficulties which were encountered; the patriotism which was manifested by the people, and the noble determination to uphold the country in her struggle, in a light that would give additional value to republican liberty.

After the adoption of the constitution of Maryland, the powers heretofore exercised by the committees ceased, and all the future exertions which the state was required to make in the common cause, were under the direction of the authority provided for by that instrument. The stirring appeals which were made by the committees, and which had had the desired effect of arousing the people to a sense of the danger which threatened their liberties, were no longer heard. The people had been summoned to the contest, and were prosecuting it with all the energy, which a just sense of the value of their rights, could command. The state government found them in this determined position, and its great duty appeared to be, to see that under their authority there should not be less zeal, less patriotism, than when these were directed by the committees. There appears to have been an apprehension entertained by many, that the state authority would not be as competent to carry on the revolution as their predecessors; and in anticipation of its failure to meet the expectations of the people, a society was formed in Baltimore, in the early part of the year 1777, to be called the "Whig Club." The objects of this society, as developed in the rules they established for their government, were such as had directed the attention of the committees, during the early part of the revolution, and when there was no controlling power in the state, either to check excesses, or to stir up reluctant spirits. But when a regular government was organized, that was supposed to be as desirous of obtaining all the benefits for the people, which were contemplated when the old government was dissolved, as had been obtained by those who had preceded them in the government of the people ; it was thought by the new state authority, that the zeal manifested by the associators of this whig club, was now an unnecessary auxiliary in the cause. Some of the rules of the club, the state considered as usurpapations of their authority, and some complaint having been preferred against them by Mr. Goddard, who had been the editor of a journal, the legislature passed a resolution, " That the governor be requested to issue his proclamation, declaring all bodies of men associating together, or meeting for the purpose, and usurping any of the powers of the government, and presuming to exercise any power over the persons or property of any subject of this state, or to carry into execution any of the laws thereof, unlawful assemblies, and requiring all such assemblies and meetings instantly to disperse." In conformity to this resolution, the governor issued a proclamation, on the 17th of April. It does not appear that this association had any other object in view, than to promote the great cause in which the state had been embarked, from the breaking out of the war, and in so doing, they thought their exertions would tend " to strengthen the bands of the present government."

Mr. Goddard, who was the complainant before the legislature, of the manner in which they had treated him, had been the editor of a journal, which had not been as friendly to those who had been exercising the authority of the province, as had been expected from one, who professed to be an advocate of the cause. His remarks on the members of the club were of a character to give offence, and they were not slow to vindicate themselves. The legislature, however, listened to Mr. Goddard, and adopted the resolution, of which we have taken notice. Mr. Goddard rather leaned to that party, which existed at this time, and which looked up to General Lee and others, as proper persons to whom the destinies of the country ought to be confided, rather than to the wise, the judicious management of General Washington, and those acting under him. Although I have no evidence that he at this time exhibited these feelings, yet I am persuaded from circumstances, that no hostility would have been manifested against him, if something of this kind had not been fastened upon him. A subsequent occasion showed the extent of his feelings towards General Lee, in such a manner, that it called forth from the friends of General Washington, such a rebuke, as had well nigh terminated in an unhappy manner.

In the month of February, of this year, (1777) a tory insurrection occurred in Somerset and Worcester counties of this state. Baltimore felt anxious to have it suppressed speedily, and for this purpose, spared neither men nor money to accomplish it. A detachment of Virginia troops, on their way to join General Washington's army in Jersey, was diverted for a time, from their original destination, and ordered for the eastern shore: They were joined by a detachment from the militia of this town, and a train of artillery from Annapolis. The whole were put under the command of Brigadier General Smallwood. The insurgents were very early dispersed, and several of the leaders were taken prisoners. This was the only instance in which the escutcheon of Maryland was blotted with such a stain, in the revolutionary contest.

I have already observed, that congress was removed to Baltimore, in December, 1776, in consequence of the near approach of General Howe's army to Philadelphia. In Baltimore, at a distance from these movements, congress could legislate without those apprehensions, which naturally tended to defeat all the purposes for which they were assembled. Here they were enabled to deliberate with the calmness and steadiness which so much befit wise and patriotic legislation. Among their first enactments here was the subject of the currency, one of those important questions, which appear to have never ceased to agitate the public mind of America, since the dawn of the revolution. The object of this present enactment was, "to require the council of safety of Pennsylvania, to take vigorous measures for punishing all such as shall refuse continental currency." Mr. Hancock, president of congress, in a letter to the council of safety of Pennsylvania, says: "The great importance to the welfare of these United States, of supporting the credit of the continental currency will suggest the propriety of the above resolve, which I am commanded by congress to transmit to you, and to request you will take measures for an immediate compliance therewith." Among the weapons which the enemies of American liberty employed to oppose it, was the effort made by them to destroy the credit of the money issued under the authority of congress. Certainly nothing contributes more to weaken the power of a nation in all her military efforts, than the destruction of her money, or the credit which represents it. The preservation of her armies in the field; the equipment of her fleets on the ocean; the peace of her people at home, all depend upon the integrity of her money and her credit. Destroy these, and her subjugation to the enemy she opposes, will soon follow. How important, then, was it to congress, to legislate upon the subject at this time. The money then used, was the only money which congress could war with. It had its value among the people, and so long as it could maintain this support, that long it was an useful agent in behalf of American rights. It was their bounden duty to protect it to the utmost, and if, in doing this, some inconvenience might be felt, it would be recollected, "that every good in this life has its alloy of evil."

There was a recommendation from congress, in March, "to the legislatures, or in their recess to the executive power of each of the United States, to cause assessments of blankets to be made, in order to furnish their several quotas of soldiers, with an article so necessary to defend themselves from the inclemency of weather and damp air, in their encampments; that all blankets to be obtained in this manner, be valued to a just and reasonable price, and paid for by the states respectively, to be repaid by the United States.

And that the legislatures, or, in their recess, the executive power, do cause money to be put into the hands of a proper officer, in every county, district, or township, in order that such blankets may be paid for, without delay or trouble to the housekeepers, on whom the assessment shall be made." As this was the first order issued by congress, having a tendency to interfere with the domestic economy of the people, it might have been supposed that its execution would have been attended with much murmuring and discontent, but I do not find any such occurred here. I find, among the documents from which I collect much of the information that I communicate, that there were many orders for blankets of a small number at a time, and even some were distributed to members of congress, for their own use. Perhaps an argument may be drawn from the scarcity of this article in this country, which, the order of congress shows did exist, in favour of the encouragement of domestic manufactures by legislative action, to supply such wants as these, which a state of war inevitably creates. The dependent state on the crown, which it was the part of British policy to exact from the colonies, necessarily required that the workshops of the colonies should be in the mother country; and so general was this sentiment in England, at the time of the enactment of the various laws which ultimately produced the revolution, that even Lord Chatham, who had so often eloquently advocated our rights, so far as taxation and representation were concerned, indignantly spurned the thought that America was to manufacture for herself. I would not permit them to make a hob nail, was the inconsistent language of this celebrated statesman. We owe it to the fostering care of a republican government, which was the creature of the revolution, that we are enabled this day to say, that we are as independent of her in all the essentials which give wealth, and comfort, and happiness to a nation, as we are of that legislation which would deny to us the common bounties of heaven.

A useful admonition was given to "printers in each of the United States," by congress, in the sitting of the 30th of December, which it may not be improper, perhaps, to preserve a memorial of, since the value of it may be highly estimated, when our country finds it necessary to put herself in the attitude and armor of war. "The printers in each of the United States, are desired to take notice, that at times when the militia have been called on to reinforce the army, the internal enemies of America have industriously circulated reports, magnifying the number of our troops in camp, and thereby prevent seasonable reinforcement. It is therefore hoped that they will, in future, avoid publishing letters or paragraphs that may have this dangerous effect, and insert this hint in each of their papers, that the yeomanry of America being apprised thereof, may at all times exert themselves when properly called on, to expel from this land an army of foreigners, that consider their customs of indiscriminately murdering, plundering, &c., to be consistent with humanity and the practices of civilized nations." Congress adjourned on the 3d of March, 1777, to meet again in Philadelphia, a few days thereafter.

It appears to have been the practice of congress, to have permitted the individual members of committees to give instructions to the various agents of congress, and to direct in what manner the various duties required of these agencies should be performed :—and the exercise of this power appears not to have been confined to the period of time in which they were attending on congress, but was equally authorized, when they were at a distance from the seat of government. Hence, many of the letters which are annexed to this narrative, were written by individual members of committees, when they were not at the seat of government. Mr. Joseph Hewes, who was a member from North Carolina, and one of the signers of the declaration of independence, appears to have been a member of the marine committee, and in that capacity communicated with Mr. Samuel Purviance. Various letters were received from him respecting the building of frigates ; the contracting for iron ; for cannon, and all the necessary equipage belonging to vessels of war. The appointments to the command of these vessels, with all the necessary officers, generally took place according to their selection. Baltimore, from its peculiar fitness for the building and equipment of vessels, was selected as one of the sites for naval constructions, and many vessels which afterwards became celebrated for the injury they inflicted on the enemy, were built here. The Virginia frigate ; the Defence sloop, Buckskin, Enterprise, Sturdy Beggar, Harlequin, Fox, &c., were among the number, and the success which sometimes attended their cruises, contributed to aid congress with the means of carrying on the war. Commodore James Nicholson was selected to command the Virginia frigate. He was a native of the eastern shore of Maryland; and gave early proofs of his peculiar fitness for the responsible station to which he was now called. He served his country faithfully during the war, and was among the number of those distinguished seamen who contributed to build up a name for his country in maritime war, which will be as imperishable as her glory. He was one of that respectable family which have been so long known in our state, and which have contributed their quota to the defence of our liberties. He was the father-in-law of the distinguished Mr. Gallatin, and died in the year 1791. Two brothers were also naval officers in the service, Capt. John Nicholson, and Capt. Samuel Nicholson. The latter became a commodore since the re-organization of the navy under the federal government, and commanded in the Mediterranean, during the cruises which took place in that sea, before and during the time of the Tripolitan war. Many letters were written by Commodore Nicholson, some of which are now published, during his command in the Chesapeake bay, to the committee of correspondence and Mr. Purviance. Before he commanded the Virginia, which was a continental ship, he commanded the ship Defence, which was a ship that had been fitted out by the province of Maryland, for the protection of the Chesapeake. His letter, acknowledging his appointment, I have already noticed.

In August, 1777, the British fleet, composed of three hundred sail of men of war, transports, &c., came to anchor just below the Bodkin point, where they continued until the next day, when they weighed anchor, and sailed for the head of Elk. This was the army under the immediate command of Sir William Howe, which ultimately reached Philadelphia. The Governor of Maryland, on the next day, issued a proclamation, requiring and commanding the county lieutenants, the field and other proper officers of the militia of the western shore of this state, immediately to march at least two full companies of each battalion of the militia, to the neighborhood of Susquehanna river, in Cecil and Harford counties, where they were to receive orders. "To defend our liberties, requires our exertions: Our wives, our children, and our country, implore our assistance. Motives amply sufficient to arm every one who can be called a man." This call was obeyed. Mr. Griffith, in his annals, says, "that the Independent company, which was commanded by Capt. John Sterett, trained as infantry, mounted their own horses, proceeded to watch the enemy on the bay side, and arrived before them at the head of it; joined the main army, including the Maryland line, near Newport; but were then ordered back by the commander in chief, to assist in protecting their homes." On the 11th of September, was fought the battle of Brandywine, at which were present the quota of troops which had been ordered out by the governor, in his proclamation of the 22d of August.

Capt. Nicholson, of the Virginia frigate, after watching the operations of the enemy, in nearly all the summer and fall of 1777, attempted to go to sea, notwithstanding the formidable obstacles which a numerous fleet presented against the success of such an attempt. On the 31st of December, he was chased by the enemy, but unfortunately struck on the middle ground, and the ship was taken. He himself escaped in his barge, but his first lieutenant, Joshua Barney, was made a prisoner. Joshua Barney was afterwards celebrated for his many naval exploits in the revolutionary war; was distinguished as a commodore in the French republican service; and in the war of his own country in 1814, gallantly sustained her honor, in his defence of the heights of Bladensburg. During Capt. Nicholson's cruise in the bay, he was constantly watching an opportunity to reach the sea. In one of his letters, relating his movements, he says: "I have had such various reports of the force of the ship that lays off the spit, both from my own officers, as well as those that have passed her, that I was determined to go down and see her myself, and returned yesterday at noon. I went into the Barrons' boat, and lay within about two miles of her half an hour, and find her to be a 32 gun frigate, which we supposed to be the Thames, and at the same time we saw another frigate between the shoe and middle ground, which I supposed to be the Emerald, and their brig and schooner tender at the North Cape. The Phenix, we understand, is cruising off the Capes. I am informed, both those frigates sail heavy, and I have sometimes thought of endeavoring to push by them, but then my preservation depends upon my sailing, which my officers, as well as myself, conclude is too great a risk."

In consequence of the approach of Sir William Howe to Philadelphia, after his victory on the Brandywine, congress removed from Philadelphia, to York in Pennsylvania. The article of salt, at all times so important in the economy of every society, became very much so in the estimation of congress, from an apprehension of its scarcity. Hence, congress never intermitted the opportunity of obtaining a supply when any circumstance presented them with the chance of securing it. A cargo of salt arrived at Baltimore, in January, 1778, and an intimation was given to congress of this fact. Immediately thereafter, an act was passed for the purpose of securing the whole for the army. Mr. Henry Laurens, who had now become the president of congress, in a letter addressed to Samuel and Robert Purviance, of 12th January, 1778, from Yorktown, says, "as some days may elapse before the governor and council can act, I am directed to transmit the copy enclosed as above mentioned, and to request you to exert your endeavors to prevent a sale or removal of the salt, until his excellency shall give directions in consequence of the present recommendation and resolve. The term "secure," in the latter part of the resolve, you may be assured, comprehends the idea of purchasing, and I have explained it to the governor. It is expected, that every friend to these states in your town, will give all needful assistance to serve the public in this momentous business; without salt, it will be impossible to lay up magazines of provisions for the army, and I need not predict what will be the consequence of deficiency." Some short time after this action of congress, salt fell here in price, for imported salt, from £18 to £7 10*s*—Country salt, from £16 to £5. This subject did not fail to excite a good deal of anxiety in the public mind, during the greater part of the war, and we shall see, in the course of our narrative, what decided steps were obliged to be taken by the people of Baltimore, to prevent the impositions which were practised in consequence of its scarcity.

The intelligence of the alliance which had taken place, between France and the United States, in virtue of the treaty entered into, between the two powers, was received in Baltimore, on the 5th of May, 1778, and in demonstration of the joy it created, the town was splendidly illuminated on the night of that day. This alliance gave a different aspect to our affairs. Wherever there was despondency, it yielded to confidence, and the contest was ever afterwards maintained, under the deep conviction, that the independence of America was established on a basis, that could only be shaken by one of those convulsions, which, in the order of providence, overturns the mightiest empires.

Congress returned to Philadelphia in July, after the British army, under General Howe, had evacuated it. As this had been the second removal of congress, in consequence of the operations of Sir William Howe, their return to it now, was never afterwards interrupted by the same cause. They remained in Philadelphia till near the close of the war, when they removed to Annapolis.

Committees of congress were in the habit of visiting places where the emergencies of the public required that large amounts should be expended in its service, as well for that of the marine as of the military. For this purpose the marine committee held a meeting in Baltimore, in the months of May and June, 1778. Their attention was directed to the minutest objects, and the care they exercised over all the interests of the public, of which they had jurisdiction, would be well worthy of the imitation of their successors. They gave a personal examination of all the means deposited in the hands of the public agents, as is instanced in the following communication.

Navy Board, Middle District,
BALTIMORE, *June 2d,* 1778.

GENTLEMEN,

We are directed by the marine committee, to take charge of the public timber, mahogany, &c., collected at this place; will therefore be obliged to you, as soon as it can conveniently be done, to furnish us with your accounts relative thereto, which will enable us with greater proficiency, to enter on this business.

We are gentlemen,
Your obedient servants,
WILLIAM SMITH,
JOHN WHARTON,
FRANCIS HOPKINSON.

To Messrs. SAMUEL & ROBERT PURVIANCE,
Baltimore.

They saw whether things, which had been required to be done by the authority of congress, was done; and if a vessel had not sailed at the time she was expected to have sailed, a reason for the delay was required to be given. When public servants thus discharge the duties required of them, the public welfare is promoted, public confidence is secured, and the approbation which is manifested by a renewal of the trust, is generally considered by such servants, as the best reward they can receive. It has often been a subject of admiration, that congress should have been enabled, with the limited means they possessed for such a purpose, to have carried on a war so long as they did, and to so triumphant an issue. It is true, that at this time, the alliance was formed with France, and the union of two such powers could not but be felt by any antagonist who should attempt to draw his sword against them. This union may, to many minds, appear to solve the mystery, and to induce the opinion that we must have succumbed to the power of Britain, but for this opportune alliance. Without depreciating in the least, the vast strength which this alliance gave us, and the weight it necessarily had in the subsequent part of the contest, we forget that we had then been waging a single handed contest with Great Britain for three years; that we had, in the mean time, captured Burgoyne with a considerable army; that Howe, after a capture of Philadelphia, had been driven from it, and through the Jerseys; that although reverses had been experienced by us, the enemy had his full share of them also. But it appears to me, one of the great secrets of our strength was in the virtue of the people. Wherever duty called, there was obedience; and no matter whether in the member of congress, who made his public duty a private concern, or in the citizen who made his private business a public concern, these exhibitions of patriotism warranted the opinion, that there was to be no peace between England and single handed America, but on the broad ground, that the United States were free, sovereign and independent. This opinion derives additional strength from the fact, that congress, in June, 1778, in rejecting the overtures made by Lord Carlisle, Sir William Eden and Governor Johnstone, the commissioners appointed by Great Britain, to settle the differences with America, say, "the only solid proof of this disposition, will be an explicit acknowledgment of the independence of these states, or the withdrawing his fleets and armies."

CHAPTER IV.

A committee of merchants was formed, at the beginning of the year 1779, whose duty it appears to have been, to provide a suitable defence for the private navigation of the Chesapeake bay. Gallies were provided, and the direction of them had been confided to Commodore Nicholson, who, a short time before, had lost the Virginia frigate, at the mouth of the Capes, in attempting to elude the vigilance of a British squadron stationed there, and who, in consequence, had no immediate command. The command of the galley Conqueror was bestowed upon him by the committee, with the approbation of the governor. The gentlemen who were united with the commodore, as officers on board this galley, deemed it proper to petition the committee on the subject of the relation which they would hold to the committee, in case of their capture. They thought it but reasonable, in case such an event should occur, that their wages should go on. They present a gloomy prospect of their situation in such a case. The horrors of a prison ship were more intimidating to them, than the cannonading of an enemy; and it was against these that they wanted some provision made; " but," in the language of a patriotism which peculiarly characterizes the seamen of America, " should we receive no address, it shall not in the least detain our services from the cause in which we are now engaged." Their petition was granted, and the Conqueror began her cruise. For three months she was stationed at and near Cape Henry, and in other parts of the bay. The protection she and the others of the squadron gave to the navigation of Baltimore, is almost incredible. Commodore Nicholson was one of those men who never flagged in any duty he undertook, and the skill with which all his maritime operations were conducted, were an earnest of that, which, in later days, has so pre-eminently characterized the American seamen.

There was published in Goddard's Maryland Jour nal of July 6th, 1779, a number of queries styled "political and military," evidently tending to bring in question the military qualifications of General Washington for the august station he then occupied; and to create a prejudice against the French nation, which, a short time before, had entered into an alliance with the United States. Among the queries which were intended to affect the character of General Washington, we select three, as samples of the general feeling of the writer towards this illustrious man.

"Whether it is salutary or dangerous, consistent with, or abhorrent from, the principles and spirit of liberty and republicanism, to inculcate and encourage in the people an idea, that their welfare, safety and glory, depend on one man? Whether they really do depend on one man?"

"Whether, amongst the late warm, or rather legal addresses, in this city, (Philadelphia) to his excellency General Washington, there was a single mortal, one gentleman excepted, who could possibly be acquainted with his merits?"

"Whether this gentleman excepted, does really think his excellency a great man, or whether evidences could not be produced of his sentiments being quite the reverse ?"

The query relative to the French nation was :

"Whether an enlightened member of a French parliament is not a thousand times more wretched than a Russian serf or peasant. As to the former, the chains, from his sensibility, must be extremely galling ; and on the latter, they fit as easy as the skin of his back ?"

On the publication of these queries, a great deal of excitement was produced against the author of them, and a demand was made for him, upon Mr. Goddard, by many citizens. Mr. Goddard at first refused to give up his name, but when he found that the citizens were determined to know who was the calumniator of the venerated chief, Mr. Goddard gave up the name of General Charles Lee as their author, and disavowed for himself, any intention to reflect on General Washington. He signed a paper of this purport : "I, William Goddard, do hereby acknowledge, that by publishing certain "queries, political and military," in the Maryland Journal, of the 6th inst., I have transgressed against truth, justice, and my duty as a good citizen ; and, in reparation, I do most humbly beg his excellency General Washington's pardon, and hope the good people of this town, will excuse my having published a piece so replete with the nonsense and malevolence of a disappointed man.

W. GODDARD."

BALTIMORE TOWN, *July 9th*, 1779."

Mr. Goddard, in a subsequent notice of this affair, ascribed the above note, which was certainly humiliating enough, to the fear he labored under from the violence of the many who required the disavowal from him; and that the moment he was relieved from the apprehension of all violence, he took the opportunity of communicating the circumstances which produced it. We are not the advocates of violence to avenge the wrong which a community may have experienced by the actions of an individual; but some apology may be found for those who, on this occasion, were desirous of shielding from insidious attacks, the fame and character of a man, who, at that time, was looked up to as the saviour of their country; knowing that if his character were then to be destroyed, the hope would depart for ever, that their country was to be free, sovereign, and independent. There was no part of America, in which the name of General Washington was held in higher veneration than in Baltimore, and there was no place where an attempt to sully it, would excite greater sensibility. In these queries, there was one of this character: "Whether, when General Howe manifestly gave over all thoughts of attacking General Washington, in the last strong position in the rear of White Plains, and fell back towards York Island, orders should not have been immediately despatched for the evacuation of Fort Washington, and for the removal of all the stores of value from Fort Lee to some secure spot, more remote from the river? Whether this was not proposed, and the proposal slighted?" General Reed, who at this time was the president of the supreme executive council of

Pennsylvania, considering himself, as so particularly alluded to in this query, felt it to be his duty not to permit the character of General Washington to be attacked through him, and "to guard the public from error in opinion," he says: "that in the fall of 1776, he was extremely anxious that Fort Washington should be evacuated. There was a difference of opinion among those whom the general consulted, and he hesitated more than he ever knew him on any other occasion, and more than he thought the public service admitted. Knowing that General Lee's opinion would be a great support to mine, I wrote to him from Hackensack, stating the case and my reasons, and I think urging him to join me in sentiment. At the close of my letter, and alluding to this, I added this sentence: 'With a thousand good and great qualities, there is a want of decision, to complete the perfect military character.' Upon this sentence, or one to this effect, wrote in haste, in full confidence, and in great anxiety for the event, is this ungenerous sentiment introduced into the world." General Lee, if not hostile before, became, after the battle of Monmouth, the undisguised enemy of General Washington, and seemed to have embraced every occasion to manifest this hostility towards him. These queries were about the first of his vindictive ebullitions, and the attempt to make them subserve his purpose in Baltimore, was met in the manner in which we have now taken notice. That Mr. Goddard had, at all times, been friendly to General Lee, had been long known, for he never concealed his feelings towards him; but that he should have taken the method he did to testify them, so as to involve the character of

Washington, was what the friends of this illustrious man could not endure; and unhappily, Mr. Goddard was made to feel the consequences of his indiscretion. The feelings which these events produced, gradually subsided, and the future intercourse of Mr. Goddard, with the people of Baltimore, was of so friendly a character, that he resumed the editorship of his paper some years after, and continued it until the year 1791, when he removed to Rhode Island, his birth place.

We have already remarked on the anxiety which congress had manifested on the subject of salt, and whilst their great desire was to secure such a supply as would be necessary for all their military purposes, they felt an anxiety to avoid its becoming an object of monopoly in the hands of speculators. This anxiety was equally felt by the people of Baltimore, and to prevent its falling into the hands of those who would thus make use of it, a society was formed for purchasing all that should be brought to market, and sell it out to the inhabitants for such a sum as would just cover the cost. The language of this association was: "We, the subscribers, inhabitants of the town and county of Baltimore, viewing with great concern, the exhorbitant price to which the article of salt has lately risen, and apprehending that the avarice of engrossers, if not speedily and vigorously opposed, will soon put that necessary of life out of the reach of the industrious poor, both in town and country, do hereby associate ourselves together, for the purpose of reducing the price of salt, and to prevent, as far as is in our power, the evil consequences which must ensue to the community at large, from the pernicious acts of speculators and engrossers.

"To attain these laudable ends, we do, each for himself, engage to pay into the hands of a treasurer, to be appointed by the society, the sums of money annexed to our respective names; this money to be expended in purchasing all the salt which may arrive at the port of Baltimore, in the course of two months; which shall be sold out in small quantities, at a price barely sufficient to repay the first cost, and defray such expenses as may necessarily attend the retailing of it. Witness our hands, this 14th of October, 1779."

S. & R. Purviance,	£10,000
William Smith,	5,000
William Neil,	4,000
Mark Pringle,	5,000
Daniel Bowley,	5,000
John McClure,	5,000
John Dorsey,	5,000
William Hammond,	4,000
Stephen Stewart,	2,000
H. D. Gough,	3,000
Thomas Langton,	1,000
Thomas Burling,	3,000
J. & T. Hollingsworth,	3,000
Hugh Young,	5,000
James Calhoun,	2,000
Jonathan Hudson,	3,000
Richard Curson,	1,000
Mark Alexander,	2,000
R. & A. McKim,	2,000
Matthew Ridley,	5,000
Amount brought forward,	£75,000

Amount brought forward,	£75,000
David Stewart,	5,000
Thomas Russell,	5,000
Hughes & Williamson,	2,000
Gardner & Gales,	2,000
John Sterret,	1,000
Samuel Smith,	2,000
Philip Graybell,	1,000
	£93,000

This society accomplished the object for which it was formed, and I find no other account of any scarcity of the article during the war.

The states of Delaware and Pennsylvania having laid an embargo on the trade of Delaware bay, so that persons residing on the waters and vicinity thereof, were prohibited the enjoyment of their accustomed trade. This was a measure that was felt very seriously in Maryland. The general assembly of Maryland authorized the governor and council to issue a proclamation, which they did, prohibiting the exportation from this state of various articles, the productions of Maryland, until the day on which the embargo in the aforementioned states would cease. This proclamation being issued the 9th of September, 1780, the duration of the embargo was until the last day of November following. This necessary retaliation on the part of Maryland, appears to have been sanctioned by the people without any murmuring or discontent.

The general assembly of Maryland passed, in the month of December, "an act for calling out of circulation the quota of this state, of the bills of credit issued by congress, and the bills of credit emitted by acts of Assembly, under the old government, and by the resolves of convention." In this law it was enacted, "after the 20th of March next, no bills of credit issued by congress, or acts of assembly during the old government, or resolves of convention, shall, within this state be deemed paper money or pass current, or be in law or equity a tender or payment for any debt, covenant, promise, contract, or agreement." "The possessors and proprietors of any of the aforesaid bills, subjects of this state, or trustees for subjects thereof, may, at any time hereafter, on or before the 1st of March next, carry into the continental loan office of this state, any of the said bills of credit, and will be entitled to receive for every forty dollars so brought in, one dollar of the new bills (emitted agreeably to the resolve of congress, of the 18th of March, and the act for sinking the quota required by congress of this state, of the bills of credit emitted by congress,) and in the same proportion for any greater quantity, and any portion after the said first day of March, and before the first day of April next, and no longer, (after which time they will be irredeemable by this state,) may bring into the said loan office, any of the said bills of credit, and be entitled to exchange them at the rate aforesaid. The commissioner is to receive no more of said continental bills of credit into his office, than, with the quantity exchanged by virtue of the said act, will amount unto twenty millions five hundred and forty dollars."

This depreciation of the paper money of America, during the strife for her liberties, was one of the ills which the people had to endure, to secure the greater good of independence. That there was murmuring at this legislative act cannot be concealed, but what was to be done? Either provide for another circulation which would have a less nominal value, but one of actual equality, with that of which it took the place, or yield to the power of England. Patriotism knew not how to make a compromise for freedom, and decided that the new emission should have the value sought to be given it by those who created it. "At a meeting of the merchants and others, inhabitants of Baltimore town, held at the Court house, on the 7th of August, 1781, to take into consideration the propriety of receiving the bills of credit emitted by an act of the last session of assembly, at par with gold and silver, James Calhoun, Esq., in the chair. It was resolved unanimously, that this town, deeply impressed with the necessity of supporting the credit of the last paper emission, as well for carrying on the operations of the present campaign with decision and vigor, as for the purposes of commerce and other necessary intercourse among the citizens of this state, will, in all their future transactions and dealings, receive the said paper money equal to specie.

"Resolved, that the following persons, viz., James Calhoun, Daniel Bowley, David McMechen, Mark Alexander, Richard Ridgely, John Dorsey, Joseph Donaldson, and John McClellan of this town; and Isaac Griest, David Stoddert, and James Tibbats of Fell's point, be a committee to call a meeting of the town, whenever they shall think an alteration of these resolves shall be necessary, or that others will be expedient to be pursued. And the said committee, or any five of them, (who are to meet on Saturday in each week) be empowered to inquire into, and hold up to public view, the conduct of all those who, regardless of our public exigencies, shall in any manner contravene these resolves, either by withholding their commodities from sale, or exacting a higher price in paper than in specie. And that the said committee be empowered to inquire into the ptices of all kinds of merchandize and country produce.

"Resolved, that the said committee be desired to have printed 150 hand bills, of the proceedings of this meeting, and transmit the same to the several counties of this state, that the measures adopted by this town, may become as public as possible.

By order,

JAMES CALHOUN, *Chairman.*

In July, 1780, the merchants of Baltimore presented a memorial to the governor and council of Maryland, representing, "that the successes of small armed vessels and boats, have invited a very formidable enemy into our bay, and that not less than twenty of their most valuable vessels, outward bound, were then blockaded up in Patuxent river, and have been for some time, and that every day they receive account of their vessels being taken or destroyed. The governor presented, in a very strong memorial to congress, these serious grievances, under which the people of Baltimore were then laboring. The governor asked for a frigate, to be stationed in the waters of the Chesapeake; but I believe it was not in the power of congress to comply with the request at that time, for I can-find no account of any frigate being stationed as was required. It appears to me, that no body of men ever watched over the interests of a community of which they were members, with a more sleepless, or intense anxiety, than did the merchants of Baltimore during the revolutionary struggle. They were among the first to suggest the measures which were necessary to be adopted to meet the crisis; they were never backward with their means, in giving efficacy to these measures; and the march of armies, the equipment of vessels of war, were accelerated by their unceasing exertions. Indeed, such was the reputation they had acquired for their patriotism abroad, that when it was determined that a detachment of troops from General Washington's army should be sent to the south, under the command of the Marquis De la Fayette, congress confided in the merchants of Baltimore, supplying them with such flour as they might want, in case of need, passing through Baltimore, which was on their way. Mr. Pickering, at that time quarter master general, and Mr. Charles Stewart, commissary general, in a letter addressed to Mr. Samuel Purviance, advising of this intended movement of the army, under the command of the Marquis, says: "We shall make no further apology at present, for giving you this trouble, as we are assured of your readiness to do essential service to your country on every occasion." The army of the Marquis came to Baltimore, on its way to Virginia, and received not only the flour which the above letter looked to have supplied here, but a considerable sum of money was raised by subscription, and paid over to him for the purpose of purchasing materials for the clothing of his army. It is due to the memory of the ladies of that day, in our town, to record the fact, that that clothing was principally made up by their fair hands. When the Marquis reached Baltimore, his destitution was not confined to the want of flour, but for nearly all the equipments, without which no army can ever be efficacious. There was but little money at that time in the state treasury, and the supply which was furnished by the patriotic gentlemen of Baltimore, is thus acknowledged in a letter from Thomas Sim Lee, Esq., governor of Maryland, addressed to Robert Purviance, Matthew Ridley and William Patterson, Esqrs.: "We very much applaud the zeal and activity of the gentlemen of Baltimore, and think their readiness to assist the executive, at a time when they were destitute of the means of providing those things, which were immediately necessary for the detachment, under the command of the Marquis De la Fayette, justly entitle them to the thanks of the public." Capt. Nicholson, whose various services in behalf of Baltimore, we have frequently noticed in this narrative, had been appointed to the command of the Trumbull frigate, and sailed from Philadelphia about the beginning of August, with a fleet which he was convoying. He was met shortly after leaving the capes of Delaware by the Iris frigate, in company with two other vessels of war, and captured. In his letter, giving an account of this capture, he says: "the Trumbull carried away her foretopmast, and his escorts abandoned him after this misfortune. A squally, rainy night came on. The enemy's squadron overhauled him; he engaged with the Iris, (notwithstanding the refusal of many of his crew to fight) until the remainder of the enemy's squadron came up, when he struck to the Iris."*

The movements of Earl Cornwallis, in August, gave reason to apprehend that he meant to make an invasion of Maryland, and possess himself of Baltimore. In consequence of this apprehension, there assembled in the town a force of about 2800 men. These came from this and adjacent counties, within two days after the alarm. Advice was soon after received, that the destination of Cornwallis was to Virginia; in consequence of which, these troops were dismissed. This was the last serious alarm which excited the people of Baltimore during the war. The events which occurred soon after in Virginia, gave a hope, that the end for which they struggled was near at hand.

In the month of September, 1781, General Washington arrived in Baltimore, on his way to Virginia, to assume the command of the combined armies of France and America, which were assembling for the purpose of putting a stop to the farther progress of Cornwallis. The Count De Rochambeau, the commander of the French army and his suite, arrived the day after General Washington; and also, the Marquis de Chastelleux, a brigadier general in the French service. These distinguished officers all left Baltimore in a day or two, to join their respective armies. An address was presented to General Washington, in behalf of the citizens of Baltimore, signed by William Smith, Samuel Purviance, John Moale, John Dorsey, and James Cal-

* It was some consolation to Capt. Nicholson to know, that a short time after his capture, the Iris was captured by Count De Grasse's squadron.

houn, in which was this beautiful sentiment: "Our prayers are for your excellency's preservation, that you may continue approved by heaven, and dreaded by tyrants; and on the restoration of public tranquillity, that you may, in peaceful retirement, enjoy that satisfaction of mind, which the sense of great and noble deeds always inspires; and may posterity, in the full possession and exercise of that freedom which your sword has assisted to establish, venerate and do ample justice to your virtues and character, to the latest ages." General Washington's reply was characterized by his usual modesty, and in conclusion, he observed: "I thank you most cordially, for your prayers and good wishes for my prosperity. May the author of all blessings aid our united exertions in the cause of liberty and universal peace. And may the particular blessings of heaven rest on you, and the worthy citizens of this flourishing town of Baltimore."

Intelligence of the surrender of Cornwallis, to the combined armies, was received at Baltimore, on the 22d of October, four days after it occurred. The following notice of this glorious event was taken in the Maryland Journal, of the 23d. "Yesterday, in consequence of intelligence, (communicated to the town by authority,) of the surrender of Earl Cornwallis, with the British army, &c. &c. &c., at York and Gloucester, to the renowned General Washington, commander in chief of the allied army, the inhabitants of this town exerted themselves, with the greatest unanimity, to celebrate this most signal victory. During the day, there were many public demonstrations of joy, (in which the gentlemen, in the military line particularly, distinguished themselves,) and in the evening, every part of the town was illuminated in the highest taste and elegance."

Soon after the surrender of Cornwallis, the Marquis De la Fayette came to Baltimore, and was received in the warmest manner by the citizens. He was addressed by them. In referring to the part he took in the campaign of Virginia, they say: "In particular, we cannot sufficiently acknowledge our sense of your late campaign in Virginia, where, with a few regulars and militia, you opposed the British commander, from whose large army and military talents, this state had such serious cause of apprehension." In reply to this part of their address, the Marquis observed: "My campaign began with a personal obligation to the inhabitants of Baltimore; at the end of it, I find myself bound to them by a new tie of everlasting gratitude." No event of the war was considered so momentous as this surrender of Cornwallis. The capture of Burgoyne was considered as an earnest of what was to be done by American soldiers, if the war were to continue. The disappointments of Howe were regarded as advantageous, because they threw a doubt over the mind of the British government, as to the successful issue of their exertions. But it was reserved for the capture of Cornwallis, to produce the conviction that Great Britain would now be compelled to declare the "rebel colonies," "free, sovereign, and independent states."

When the intelligence of this surrender reached England, parliament determined that they would support the war no longer. Mr. Fox, who had at all times been friendly to American rights, declared what he now wanted, was a substantial connexion with America. Mr. Rigby said, "it was as idle to talk of the sovereignty of Britain over America, as it was to add the title of king of France, to that of his sovereign's other titles. He held other doctrines, he said, at another time, and his principles were still the same, but time and *accident* had altered the system of things." He called upon Mr. Fox, to know what he meant by his words, 'substantial connexion with America.' Mr. Fox answered, "by these words he meant, no act of sovereignty to be exercised by Great Britain over America, but such a substantial connexion as should be derived from mutual interest, like that subsisting between Portugal and Britain."

On the 13th of June, 1782, a proclamation from Thomas Sim Lee, Esq., governor of Maryland, was issued, announcing the birth of a Dauphin of France, and appointing the 25th of the same month, as the day for the celebration of the auspicious event. "And I cannot doubt," says the governor, "that the citizens of this state will unite in the joy which an occasion so nearly affecting the happiness of our ally, will not fail to inspire, while they experience a new source of satisfaction on the birth of a prince, from whom we have every reason to expect a continuance of the blessings of our alliance. The same lively attention to the injured and oppressed, and all those great and good qualities, which have excited our admiration and gratitude, and which so eminently distinguished his illustrious father." The day selected by the proclamation, was celebrated in Baltimore. There was an elegant dinner provided at a place called the Independent Spring, at which were present, the

Chevalier D'Anmour, the French consul, and a number of strangers and French gentlemen. After dinner, many toasts were drank, and the entertainment was closed with that harmony and good humor, which, in a peculiar manner, distinguished the day.

The first toast drank, was, "the Dauphin of France." What a distressing thought arises at the recollection of this name and this association! This young prince, born to the most splendid inheritance which man can covet; apparently destined to fill a throne, which had resisted the assaults of eight hundred years; the short space of eleven years saw this mighty fabric overturned by those who ought to have been its supporters; his father perish on a scaffold, and himself placed in one of the humblest occupations for a maintenance: but a short time after this awful change, his very being was covered with a pall of darkness that still rests over it.

The French forces, under Count Rochambeau, arrived in Baltimore, about the 22d of July, on their return from the capture of Cornwallis. They consisted of upwards of five thousand men. They departed from Baltimore for the north, about the 23d of August. There were two addresses presented by the merchants of Baltimore to Count Rochambeau; the one, on his return from Virginia; the other, on his departure with his troops. The address presented on his return, offers the "most sincere thanks, in this public manner, for the distinguished aid and protection, which you have from time to time, so willingly afforded to the commercial interests of this state, and to inform your excellency, that we are happy in the opportunity of paying you this tribute, so justly due to distinguished merit."

The reply of Count Rochambeau, to this part of the address is thus expressed : "The intention of the king my master, towards his faithful allies, being, that his auxiliary troops should not only protect the liberties of the United States, but watch over their commercial interests, as often and as much as it would be in their power. I have felt a peculiar pleasure to have been able to render some service to your state. The noblest reward for me is, without doubt, the approbation of such a respectable body of citizens. I embrace with pleasure, gentlemen, this occasion to render you my sincere thanks for the readiness with which you have taken in your houses our staff officers and others, whose duty and station render the convenience of a house absolutely necessary to them." Count Rochambeau embarked at Annapolis for France, on the 8th of January, 1783. The news of peace reached Baltimore, on the 25th of March, 1783.

I have thus detailed the principal events connected with the revolutionary war, which occurred in Baltimore town, and which I have supposed would excite any particular interest at the present day. They certainly were events, which at the time they occurred, were considered as having an important bearing on the great question then at issue, and of which, those who were immediately instrumental in their occurrence, cherished their recollection as among the most valuable incidents of the revolution. The contest, as waged by our infant town, presents as striking an instance of patriotism, as the history of our country shews. Our people were among the first to resent the outrages of England as exhibited in the various taxations which she had levied on the colonies. They were also among the first to stir up the colonies in the south, to a just indignation of these wrongs; and when the war actually took place, although Maryland was nearly exempt from any visitations of the enemy, yet that did not prevent Baltimore from furnishing her quota of officers and troops, who, under the proud name of the "old Maryland line," did honor to the cause they aided, and to the people from whom they were sent. It is a grateful duty now to take notice of the names of some of these gentlemen, and to offer to those of the present day, who are called upon to sustain their country's honor, such an example, which, if imitated, will secure to themselves unfading glory.

General Otho Holland Williams, was a native of Prince George's county. As early as 1775, he had the command of a company, which marched to Boston. At the attack on Fort Washington, he was wounded, and fell into the hands of the enemy. He was at this time a major. From the treatment he received from the enemy, his health became so seriously affected, that, during his life, he never recovered it. He was promoted to the command of the sixth regiment of the Maryland line, during his captivity, and on being released from it, he marched with his regiment to the south, and in all the battles fought by that celebrated line, he distinguished himself. He acted as deputy adjutant general of the southern army, under General Gates, and was in the disastrous battle of Camden. A remnant of the defeated army was formed into two battalions, constituting a regiment, and the command of it was given to Col. Williams and Lieut. Col.

Howard. When General Green joined the army, he appointed Col. Williams adjutant general. In the battle at the Eutaw Springs, he gained the highest honors. Near the close of the war, as a reward for his services, he was promoted by congress to the rank of brigadier general. About a year before the close of the war, he retired from the military service, and was appointed by the state, naval officer for the port of Baltimore, in the room of Mr. Sollers, who had died at this time. He held this office until the organization of the federal government, in 1789, when he was appointed collector of this port by General Washington. He died in July, 1794.

General Mordecai Gist, was born in Baltimore county, and when the war first broke out, he was appointed a major in a regiment of regular troops. He remained with his regiment, which was stationed at Baltimore, for some time after its formation. It was afterwards marched to the north, and served in the campaigns of the northern army. Major Gist was considered so meritorious an officer, that he was soon promoted to the rank of a colonel; and when the Maryland line was sent to the south, he also went as a brigadier general. He continued in the service, an active and meritorious officer, until the peace. After the peace, he married in South Carolina, and died there in 1791.

Col. John E. Howard, was a native of Baltimore county. He entered the army as a captain, and in the battle of the White Plains, he became distinguished. When a number of battalions were required to be raised by a resolve of congress, Capt. Howard was appointed a major in one of the number allotted to Maryland. He was with the army at Rocky Hill, near Princeton, in April, 1777, and remained with it until June, when he returned home for awhile in consequence of the death of his father. He rejoined the army in September following, and was in the battle of Germantown. In June, 1779, Major Howard received the commission of lieutenant colonel of the 5th Maryland regiment. He was in the disastrous battle of Camden, but that portion of duty assigned to Col. Howard in the battle, was sustained with great gallantry. In December, subsequent to the battle, General Green arrived, and took command of the southern army. In January, 1781, was fought the battle of the Cowpens. The glories of that day, belong principally to Col. Howard. At Eutaw, he had the command of the second regiment. Col. Howard, on this occasion, again distinguished himself, and at this time he received a severe wound in the left shoulder. General Green observed of him, in one of his letters, "Col. Howard was as good an officer as the world afforded, and deserved a statue of gold, no less than the Roman and Grecian heroes." In Nov. 1788, Col. Howard was chosen governor of Maryland, and continued in the executive chair for three years. In the year 1796, he was elected a senator of the United States, in which situation he continued until the year 1803. He died in 1827.

General Samuel Smith was born in Carlisle, Pennsylvania, but came to Baltimore in childhood. At the breaking out of the war, he was appointed a captain in one of the regular companies stationed in Baltimore, but rose soon after to the rank of colonel. In this character he joined the army, at that time, watching the movements of Sir William Howe, near Philadelphia. He was stationed, with a part of his regiment, at Mud Fort, on the Delaware, when the British fleet were ascending that river. His gallant defence of that fort, won him the reputation of a skilful and gallant officer, and as a testimonial of his bravery, congress presented him with a sword. He retired from the army some time after this battle, but did not withdraw from the service of his country. In Baltimore, he took command of a regiment of militia, and continued doing duty in this command during the whole of the war. General Smith, some years after the war, was elected to the legislature of the state, where he remained until he was elected to congress, in the year 1792. In congress, he continued until the year 1833, having served forty years in the national councils, with an intermission of only six weeks, during that long period. General Smith, in the year 1793, was made a brigadier general, and in that capacity commanded a brigade from Maryland, in the expedition of 1794, to suppress what was called the whiskey insurrection, in the western parts of Pennsylvania. As major general of the third division of Maryland militia, he was entrusted with the defence of Baltimore, during the war of 1812. The repulse of the British army, in its attack upon Baltimore, was the result of his judicious management of the campaign. At the age of eighty-three years, he was called upon by his fellow citizens to exercise the arduous duties of mayor of the city of Baltimore. Those duties he performed for three years, and then retired. He died a few months thereafter, and the city of Baltimore did honor to herself, by giving to his remains a public burial.

It may not be out of place to notice the services of some gentlemen in civil employments, which were not the less valuable from the absence of military glare. They served their country faithfully, and their memories are worthy of a place in the recollections of a posterity, who are in the uninterrupted enjoyment of rights they contributed to transmit to them. Mr. David Stewart was appointed by congress to discharge the duties of marshall, for the state of Maryland. These duties were performed with a zeal that seems to have been peculiar to the patriots of those days. This occupation was no sinecure, as indeed were none of the offices created by congress. When the war was over, Mr. Stewart resumed his commercial business, and united himself in it with Mr. David Plunket. He continued in that connexion, until the unfortunate loss of Mr. Plunket, at sea, in the year 1793. Mr. Stewart died in 1817.

Mr. Plunket was an active partizan officer, and had been in several battles. He was by birth an Irish gentlemen, and the elder brother of the present Lord Plunket, late the chancellor of Ireland. He was the person employed by the committee of 1776, to wait on congress, to receive from them the instruction that might be given respecting the seizure of the person of Governor Eden.

Mr. Robert Purviance was, with his brother Mr. Samuel Purviance, appointed by congress, as an agent in the management of such concerns as were entrusted to them by their legislation. These were of a most various and multiplied character, and demanded the whole time and labor of those who had charge of them.

On the adoption of the constitution of the United States, when the new government went into operation, General Washington appointed Mr. Purviance the naval officer of the port of Baltimore, and on the death of General Williams, who had been at the same time appointed the collector, he made him the collector, which office he held until his death, in October, 1806. I do not violate the sanctity of private correspondence, when I say, that these offices, thus bestowed, were a testimonial of approbation for revolutionary services.

Mr. David Poe acted as a quarter master throughout the whole of the war. He was a faithful officer, and was held in great estimation by all who had business to transact with him. Such was his devotion to his country, that it was almost proverbial; and so unabated was it, long after the peace was proclaimed, that by the public sentiment, he became a brevetéd general, and in his latter days, was better known as General Poe, than by any other name.

APPENDIX.

No. 1.

Boston, August 11*th*, 1768.

Gentlemen,—The merchants and traders in this town, sensibly affected with the late acts of Parliament, imposing duties on sundry articles of commerce, with the express view of raising a revenue out of America; and with the embarrassments and restrictions the trade thereby at present labors under, are fully convinced of the necessity of exerting themselves, without any further delay, in a firm, but peaceable manner, for obtaining relief. They have, therefore, lately had a meeting, and opened a subscription, which was soon filled up by the merchants in general, wherein they engage to and with each other, as follows:

1st. That they will not send for, or import from Great Britain, either upon their own accounts, or upon commission this fall, any other goods than what are already ordered for the fall supply.

2d. That they will not send for, ori mport any kind of goods or merchandize from Great Britain, either on their own accounts, or on commissions, or any otherwise, from the first of January, 1769, to the first of January, 1770, except salt, coals, fish hooks and lines, hemp, duck, bar lead, shot, wool cards, and hard wire.

3d. That they will not purchase of any factor, or others, any kind of goods imported from Great Britain, from January, 1769, to January, 1770.

4th. That they will not import on their own account, or on commissions or purchase, of any who shall import from any other colony in America, from January, 1769, to January, 1770, any tea, glass, paper, or other goods commonly imported from Great Britain.

5th. That they will not, from and after the first day of January, 1769, import into this province, any tea, paper, glass, or painter's colours, until the act imposing duties on these articles shall be repealed.

The merchants here have been for some time thoroughly convinced of the importance and necessity of the measure, and they have lately been confirmed in their sentiments by letters from their friends in England, who have given it as their opinion, that such a procedure would undoubtedly be attended with success, and indeed it is natural to expect it. Petitions and remonstrances will be of little force with those whose interest they oppose, but make it their interest, and they will soon attend to them ; feeling will bring conviction, and conviction will increase our friends and advocates. You'll please to observe, that the merchants, here have entered into this agreement without any conditions however. At a time when uncommon measures are taking to prevent parliamentary application, they cannot but persuade themselves, that the merchants in all the other colonies are clearly convinced of the necessity of uniting in the cause of liberty. They are confident, therefore, that the merchants with you, will cheerfully and unanimously co-operate with us in the lawful, prudent, and salutary measure, especially when they consider that upon their concurrence, their speedy concurrence, greatly depends the success of the measures entered into by the merchants of this town.

We are appointed a committee, by the merchants, to correspond with the merchants in the other colonies, relative to the embarrassments the trade may at any time labor under, and should be glad to hear from you, as soon as the merchants with you have come into any resolutions relative to the subject of this letter.

We are, with respect,

Your most obedient humble servants,

Thomas Cushing,
John Hancock,
John Rowe,
John Erving, Jr.
Edward Payne,
William Phillips,
John Barrett.

To Samuel and Robert Purviance, Esqrs., Baltimore.

No. 2.

Boston, May 13th, 1774.

Gentlemen,—I am desired by the freeholders and other inhabitants of the town, to enclose you an attested copy of their vote, passed in town meeting, legally assembled this day. The occasion of this meeting is most alarming. We have received the copy of an act of the British parliament (which is also enclosed) wherein it appears, that the inhabitants of this town have been tried and condemned, and are to be punished by the shutting up of the harbor and other ways, without their having been even accused of any crime committed by them; for no such crime is alleged in the act.

11

The town of Boston is now suffering the stroke of vengeance, in the common cause of America. I hope they will sustain the blow with a becoming fortitude; and that the effects of this cruel act, intended to intimidate and subdue the spirits of *all* America, will, by the joint efforts *of all*, be frustrated.

The people receive this edict with indignation. It is expected by their enemies, and feared by some of their friends, that this town singly, will not be able to support the cause under so severe a trial. As the very being of every colony, considered as a free people, depends upon the event, a thought so dishonorable to our brethren cannot be entertained, as that this town will now be left to struggle alone.

General Gage is just arrived here, with a commission to supersede Governor Hutchinson. It is said that the town of Salem, about twenty miles east of this metropolis, is to be the seat of government:—that the commissioners of the customs and their numerous retinue, are to remove to the town of Marblehead, a town contiguous to Salem, and that this, if the general shall think proper, is to be a garrisoned town. Reports are various and contradictory.

I have the honor to subscribe, in behalf of the town of Boston, Gentlemen,

Your most humble servant,

SAMUEL ADAMS.

As this town has not the pleasure of a political correspondence with any gentleman in Maryland, I beg the favor of Mr. William Lux of Baltimore, to permit me to address this letter to him, to be communicated as his wisdom shall dictate. And a letter from him will very much oblige his

Most humble servant,

SAMUEL ADAMS.

To Mr. William Lux, merchant, Baltimore.

No. 3.

At a meeting of the freeholders and other inhabitants of the town of Boston, legally qualified and named in publick town meeting, assembled at Fanueil hall, on Friday, the 13th day of May, 1774. Voted, that it is the opinion of this town, that if the other colonies come into a joint resolution to stop all importations from Great Britain, and exportations to Great Britain, and every part of the West Indies, till the act for blocking up this harbor be repealed, the same will prove the salvation of North America and her liberties. On the other hand, if they continue their exports and imports, there is high reason to fear, that fraud, power, and the most odious oppression, will rise triumphant over right, justice, social happiness and freedom. And moreover; that this vote be forthwith transmitted by the moderator to all our sister colonies, in the name and behalf of this town. Attest,

WILLIAM COOPER, *Town Clerk.*

No. 4.

Philadelphia, May 21st, 1774.

Gentlemen,—You will, no doubt, before the receipt of this, have a copy of the act of parliament, for shutting up the port of Boston, on account of the destruction of the tea sent out by the East India company, and we know that you consider them as sufferers in the general cause of America. What part you may think it your duty to act on the present alarming occasion, we must leave to your own wisdom, and that you may be the better enabled to come to a determination, we take the liberty to enclose you copies of the papers which we received from Boston, and also copies of a resolve passed by a number of the inhabitants of this city last evening, and of the letter we sent to the town of Boston, enclosing the same. We shall be glad, by the first opportunity, to know the result of your deliberations on this interesting business, and are with great regard,

Gentlemen,

Your most humble servants,

JOHN DICKINSON,

WILLIAM SMITH,

In behalf, and by order of the committee of correspondence.

To Dr. Stevenson, Messrs. Samuel Purviance, Alexander Lawson, and others, principal gentlemen in Baltimore.

No. 5.

Philadelphia, May 21st, 1774.

Gentlemen,—We have received your very interesting letter, together with a letter from the town of Boston, and the vote they have passed on the present alarming occasion, and such measures have been pursued thereon, as the shortness of the time would allow; to collect the sense of this large city, is difficult, and when their sense is obtained, they must not consider themselves as authorised to judge or act for this populous province, in a business so deeply interesting as the present is to all British America.

A very respectable number of the inhabitants of this city was, however, assembled last evening, in order to consult what was proper to be done, and after reading the sundry papers you transmitted to us, and also a letter from the committee of correspondence of New York, the enclosed resolves were passed, in which you may be assured we are sincere, and that you are considered as now suffering in the general cause.

But what further advice to offer on this sad occasion is a matter of great difficulty, which not only requires more mature deliberations, but also that we should take the necessary means to obtain the general sentiments of our fellow inhabitants of this province, as well as of our sister colonies. If satisfying the East India company for the damages they have sustained, would put an end to this unhappy controversy, and leave us on the footing of constitutional liberty for the future, it is presumed, that neither you nor we could continue a moment in doubt what part to act, for it is not the value of the tax, but the indefeasible right of giving and granting our own money from which we can never recede, that is the matter now in consideration.

By what means the truly desirable circumstance of a reconciliation and future harmony with our mother country, on constitutional grounds, may be obtained, is indeed a weighty question. Whether by the method you have suggested of a non-importation and non-exportation agreement, or by a general congress of deputies, from the different colonies, clearly to state what we conceive our rights, and make a claim or petition of them to his majesty, in firm, but decent and dutiful terms, so as that we may know by what line to conduct ourselves in future, are now the great points to be determined. The latter method, we have reason to think, would be most agreeable to the people of this province, and the first step that ought to be taken; the former may be reserved as our last resource, should the other fail, which we trust will not be the case, as many wise and good men, in the mother country, begin to see the necessity of a good understanding with the colonies upon the general plan of liberty, as well as commerce. We shall endeavor, as soon as possible, to collect the sentiments of the people of this province, and the neighboring colonies, on these grand questions, and should also be glad to know your sentiments thereon. In the meantime, with sincere fellow feeling for your sufferings, and great regard to your persons, we are

Your very humble servants,

John Dickinson,
William Smith,

And others, in behalf, and by order of
the committee of correspondence.

To the committee of correspondence, in the town of Boston.

No. 6.

At a meeting of a number of respectable inhabitants of the city of Philadelphia, on Friday, the 20th of May, 1774,

It was resolved, that John Dickinson, Dr. William Smith, Edward Pennington, John Nesbitt, Samuel Howell, Thomas Mifflin, Joseph Read, Thomas Wharton, Jr., Benjamin Marshall, Joseph Moulder, Thomas Barclay, George Clymer, Charles Thomsen, Jeremiah Warder, Jr., John Cox, John Gibson, be a committee to correspond with our sister colonies, until some alteration is made in this appointment, by a more general meeting of the inhabitants of the said city.

That the said committee be instructed to apply to the governor, to call the assembly of the province.

That the said committee be instructed to write our friends the people of Boston, informing them that we truly feel for their unhappy situation; that we recommend to them firmness, prudence and moderation, and that we shall continue to evince our firm adherence to the cause of American liberty.

And that the committee do also inform our brethren in New York, and the other colonies, of the above resolutions.

No. 7.

Baltimore, 25th May, 1774.

Gentlemen,—Yesterday we received by express, a letter from the committee of correspondence, at Philadelphia, enclosing the vote of the town of Boston, copy of a letter from Boston to the gentlemen of Philadelphia, and the reply thereto, &c. A meeting of the principal inhabitants of this town was unanimously called, and the papers read, in order to collect, in some measure, as well as so sudden an occasion would admit, the general sense of the people, on a subject so very alarming and interesting to every American. The result was, that we appointed a committee to correspond with the gentlemen of the other colonies, who may write us on this, or any other public matter: and more particularly to correspond with you and any other towns in our own province, with a view, if possible, to collect the public sense of a measure, in which none of us can be indifferent.

It has been proposed to call a general meeting of the gentlemen of the county at large, to collect their opinion, whether it might not be expedient to apply to the governor, to convene the assembly on this occasion. But that, as well as a reply to the committee of Philadelphia, we judged proper to postpone until we should consult with you. It would give us great pleasure to harmonize with you and all our brethren, through the province, in the present crisis, and we shall be glad to know your sentiments as soon as possible. We are, with the greatest respect,

Gentlemen,

Your most humble servants.

Signed by order, and in behalf of the committee,

SAMUEL PURVIANCE, Jr.

WILLIAM BUCHANAN.

The committee appointed for this town, are, Andrew Buchanan, Robert Alexander, William Smith, John Smith, John Moale, William Buchanan, William Lux, Thomas Harrison, Dr. John Boyd, Robert Christie, Sr., Isaac Van Bibber, Samuel Purviance, Jr.

To the gentlemen of Annapolis.

No. 8.

Annapolis, May 26th, 1774.

Gentlemen,—We feel the most sensible pleasure, in the receipt of your letter, by the hands of Mr. Alexander. Nothing can be plainer, than that the suffering of Boston, is in the general cause of America, and that union and mutual confidence is the basis on which our common liberties can only be supported. We enclose you a copy of a letter wrote to Virginia, and of the resolutions past yesterday in our town meeting. It appears to us that much depends on the determinations of Virginia, which we shall anxiously expect. Unanimity in the Massachusetts, New York, Maryland, Virginia and South Carolina, which may reasonably be expected, bids fair for success. We cheerfully accept your invitation, to a free intercourse, and shall most gladly harmonize with you in all possible measures, for the general good.

We are, gentlemen,

With the utmost sincerity and respect,

Your most obedient servants,

J. Hall, William Paca,
Charles Carroll, Samuel Chase,
Thomas Johnson, Jr. Mr. Hammond, absent.

To Messrs. Samuel Purviance, Jr., William Buchanan, Andrew Buchanan, and the other gentlemen who compose the committee of correspondence in Baltimore town.

No. 9.

At a meeting of the inhabitants of the city of Annapolis, on Wednesday, the 25th day of May, 1774, after notice given of the time, place, and occasion of this meeting:

Resolved, that it is the unanimous opinion of this meeting, that the town of Boston is now suffering in the common cause of America, and that it is incumbent on every colony in America, to unite in effectual means to obtain a repeal of the late act of parliament, for blocking up the harbor of Boston.

That it is the opinion of this meeting, that if the colonies come into a joint resolution to stop all importations from, and all exportations to Great Britain, till the said act be repealed, the same will preserve North America and her liberties.

Resolved, therefore, that the inhabitants of this city will join in an association with the several counties of this province, and the principal colonies in America, to put an immediate stop to all exports to Great Britain, and that, after a short day hereafter, to be agreed on, that there be no imports from Great Britain, till the said act be repealed, and that such association be on oath.

That it is the opinion of this meeting, that the gentlemen of the law of this province, bring no suits for the recovery of any debt, due from any inhabitant of this province, to any inhabitant of Great Britain, until the said act be repealed.

That the inhabitants of this city will, and it is the opinion of this meeting, that this province ought, immediately to break off all trade and dealings with that colony or province, who shall refuse or decline to come into similar resolutions with a majority of the colonies.

That Messrs. John Hall, Charles Carroll, Thomas

Johnson, Jr., William Paca, Matthias Hammond, and Samuel Chase, be a committee for this city, to join with those who shall be appointed for Baltimore town, and other parts of this province, to constitute one general committee, and that the gentlemen appointed for this city, immediately correspond with Baltimore town, and other parts of this province, to effect such association as will best secure American liberty.

No. 10.

Annapolis, 25*th May*, 1774.

Gentlemen,—We this morning received a letter from the committee of correspondence of Philadelphia, enclosing their resolutions, with a copy of a letter, and a vote of the town of Boston. We esteem it a very lucky circumstance, that your general assembly is now sitting, as it affords so good an opportunity of instantly collecting the sense of your colony on a point, on which the liberties of America must turn; and was it not absolutely necessary, that measures should be instantly taken, we should have waited with pleasure your resolutions, which we cannot doubt will be found on the same generous principle, which have hitherto actuated your colony on every late attempt against American liberty. That no time may be lost, we shall communicate the papers transmitted to us to every part of our province, and endeavor to give the strongest impressions of the sufferings of Boston, in the common cause. We shall anxiously expect your resolutions, in the mean time, we propose the sense of the people to be taken at their meetings, on the following heads.

1st. That an immediate stop be put to all exports to Great Britain, and that after a short day to be agreed on, there be no importation from Great Britain, till the act for blocking up the harbor of Boston be repealed.

2d. That the association be on oath.

3d. That the gentlemen of the law, in this province, bring no suit for the recovery of any debt, due from any inhabitant of this province, to any inhabitant of Great Britain, until the said act be repealed.

4th. That this province will immediately break off all trade and dealings with that colony or province, which shall refuse or decline to come into similar resolutions with a majority of the colonies.

We have the most sanguine hope that Maryland will cheerfully co-operate with your colony, to any extent of non-importation or non-exportation. We expect committees will be appointed as soon as possible; through which we hope a cordial and free intercourse will be established, between your colony and our province, and that the value and consequence of those colonies to Great Britain, will be demonstrated by withholding our tobacco.

We are gentlemen,

Your most obedient servants,

C. Carroll, Samuel Chase,
J. Hall, Matthias Hammond,
Thomas Johnson, Jr. Stephen West.
William Paca,

To the Honorable Peyton Randolph, Esq., and other gentlemen of Williamsburg.

No. 11.

To the freeholders and gentlemen of Baltimore county:

Gentlemen,—On Tuesday last, we received (by express) a letter from the committee of correspondence at Philadelphia, enclosing a letter from the town of Boston, on the very alarming situation of their affairs, by the late act of parliament, for blocking up the harbor of said place: also, a copy of certain resolves entered into by the gentlemen of Philadelphia, in consequence thereof. A meeting of the principal inhabitants of this place was immediately held, in order to consult what measures we ought to take, in a matter so very interesting to every American. A committee, (whereof we are the members) was appointed, with directions to correspond with any committees instituted in our own, or the neighboring colonies, in order to collect the public sense, and promote, in a peaceable and orderly manner, the most effectual measures for obtaining relief to our fellow subjects, suffering in the common cause of America.

In consequence of this appointment, we yesterday wrote a letter to the gentlemen of Annapolis, acquainting them, we judge it expedient, to collect the sense of the gentlemen of our county at large, on a subject so interesting to every individual. To this, we received a friendly reply, (by express) this morning, with assurances from the gentlemen of Annapolis, that the members of their committee will be here against Tuesday next, in order to confer with the gentlemen of this county, on this important subject.

Permit us, therefore, to request, that as many of the

principal gentlemen and freeholders, (as conveniently can) will be so kind as to favor us with their company and advice, at the Court house in this town, at 2 o'clock on Tuesday next, which will be highly acceptable to their and the public's

Very humble servants,

ANDREW BUCHANAN,	WILLIAM SMITH,
ROBERT ALEXANDER,	THOMAS HARRISON,
WILLIAM BUCHANAN,	WILLIAM LUX,
ROBERT CHRISTIE, Sr.	JOHN BOYD,
JOHN MOALE,	JOHN SMITH,
ISAAC VAN BIBBER,	SAMUEL PURVIANCE, Jr.

Baltimore Town, May 27th, 1774.

No. 12.

Baltimore, May 27th, 1774.

Gentlemen,—We are highly pleased with the generous zeal you are pleased to express for the liberties of our country, so violently invaded by the late act of parliament. It will animate us, (and, we trust, every other part of the province) in adopting the most effectual means of providing relief for our suffering brethren of Boston, when we see the metropolis of the province, and so many gentlemen of distinguished abilities, so warmly disposed to co-operate with us. At a meeting of our committee, we have just now agreed to circulate a printed address to the principal gentlemen and freeholders of this county, inviting them to meet us at the Court house, at 2 o'clock on Tuesday next: and in confidence of what Mr. Alexander has mentioned, shall venture to promise them the pleasure of seeing some gentlemen of your committee here, to confer with them on this interesting occasion.

We yesterday forwarded copies of the papers received from Philadelphia, to the gentlemen of Norfolk and Portsmouth, in Virginia, and to the gentlemen of Alexandria, hoping, by a discovery of our zeal in the common cause, to beget the same disposition in our neighboring friends. By a gentleman just come from Williamsburgh, which he left last Saturday, we learn, the gentlemen of that place were impatiently expecting an express from Philadelphia, and express great desire of taking some public measures on this occasion. We are, with much respect, gentlemen,

Your most humble servants,

SAMUEL PURVIANCE, Jr. WILLIAM SMITH,
JOHN SMITH, JOHN MOALE.
WILLIAM BUCHANAN,

To the committee of correspondence at Annapolis.

No. 13.

Baltimore, 25*th May*, 1774.

Gentlemen,—On Tuesday last, we received, by express, from Philadelphia, a letter from the committee of correspondence, at that place, enclosing a copy of the vote of the town of Boston, a letter from said town to the gentlemen of Philadelphia, advising of their present unhappy situation, and requesting their brotherly advice on so interesting an occasion; copies of which vote and letter, the reply thereto, and the resolves entered into at Philadelphia, we now take the liberty of communicating to you, not doubting your readiness to take a friendly part in a matter so interesting to every American.

On receipt of those papers, we immediately convened the principal inhabitants of this place, in order to collect, in some measure, their sense of the matter. The result was, that we appointed a committee, (of which you have the names annexed) to correspond with the committees of any neighboring colonies, who may consult us on this, or any other public occasion, and particularly to promote a general correspondence of sentiments with our brethren through this province, in such measures as may, on mature consideration, be thought most advisable to take, on this alarming occasion. It has been proposed to convene the principal gentlemen of our county at large, in order to promote an application for calling the assembly of the province, but that we have postponed for the present, until we have the advice of our friends in Annapolis on the matter.

We hope and expect, that the gentlemen of your province, who distinguished themselves as the foremost in asserting the cause of American liberty, and opposing the scheme of parliamentary taxation, will now exert themselves with spirit and boldness in the cause of Boston, now so violently attacked for defending the common cause of America: and we doubt not that the gentlemen of your town in particular, will heartily concur in whatever measures may best serve the general good. We are, with much respect, gentlemen,

Your most humble servants,

In behalf of the committee,

SAMUEL PURVIANCE, Jr.
WILLIAM BUCHANAN.

The committee of correspondence of Baltimore town: Andrew Buchanan, William Smith, John Smith, John

Moale, William Buchanan, William Lux, Thomas Harrison, Robert Christie, Sr., Robert Alexander, Dr. John Boyd, Isaac Van Bibber, Samuel Purviance, Jr.

To the gentlemen of Alexandria.

No. 14.

Gentlemen,—At 4 o'clock this afternoon, I arrived here, and immediately delivered your letter to Mr. Johnson, one of the committee of correspondence, appointed for this city. A meeting was immediately held, of all the gentlemen who compose that committee, before whom your letter was laid. As it is with great pleasure, I can assure you, that the letter and conduct of our town, gave great satisfaction, and dissipated a gloom from the countenances of the gentlemen, occasioned by a report, that Baltimore town was lukewarm in the cause, and would not adopt any measures beyond that of a congress. What has been done here, you can best collect from the papers, which the gentlemen now enclose you by express, with an answer to your letter. I have only, for my part, to request, that hand bills may be immediately circulated, as proposed, to call a meeting of the county, on Tuesday next, at which time the gentlemen of the committee from Annapolis propose to be in our town, that some joint effort may be made to rouse the Philadelphians to a sense of that danger, which now threatens American liberty. The committee here, are transmitting copies of all their letters and proceedings to each city of this province, and I could wish, if you think it expedient, that letters from our town, signifying your appointment, might also be forwarded as early as possible. Baltimore town, considered in a commercial view, is, with great justness, esteemed the place of most consequence in the province, and coinciding in sentiment with the metropolis, may have a happy effect on the whole. The spirit of liberty is certainly contagious; I feel the force of the observation most sensibly at this present moment; and however warm I might appear to some of the —— —— of our town, I don't find that I went an inch beyond the sentiments of the gentlemen of this place, nor further than what every honest American ought to go. The messenger being ready, I conclude in haste,

Your humble servant,

R. ALEXANDER.

Annapolis, Thursday, 6 *o'clock, P. M., May* 26*th*, 1774.

The committee here propose writing to New York and Boston, by the post, on Saturday. They will defer writing to Philadelphia until after Saturday, when they expect to be in Baltimore town.

To the committee of correspondence, Baltimore town.

No. 15.

Alexandria, May 29*th*, 1774.

Gentlemen,—After acknowledging the receipt of your letter, with the several papers enclosed, we have to inform you, that following the good example you had shewn us, we called a meeting of the principal inhabitants of this town, who determined upon the choice of a committee, for carrying on such a correspondence, as we judged necessary for conveying our sentiments to the neighboring towns.

Notwithstanding the anxiety we felt for the unhappy situation of Boston, groaning under the lash of arbitrary power, in the cause of all America, we determined to wait for the exertion of the well known spirit of our assembly, at that time sitting, as we apprehended, before we entered into any determination, with regard to our conduct, at this alarming crisis.

We are still obliged, in some measure, to wait the determination of our late representatives, though not in their legislative capacity. The governor, after their passing an order, (a copy of which we enclose you,) for setting apart the first day of June, as a day of fasting, humiliation and prayer, having dissolved them.

They are determined to keep the day in the manner they proposed, and after that, it is expected will enter into some spirited associations, for procuring, as far as lies in their power, some relief for their distressed brethren in New England. We shall be much obliged, by your friendly information, from time to time, of any emergencies which may occur of general concernment, and are, gentlemen, with much respect and regard, in behalf of the committee,

Your most obedient servants,

John Carlyle, William Rumney,
William Ramsay, Robert H. Harrison,
John Dalton, John Harper.

List of the committee from the town of Alexandria: John Carlyle, William Ramsay, John Dalton, Dr. William Rumney, Robert Adam, James Kirk, James Hendricks, Robert H. Harrison, George Gilpen, John Harper.

To Messrs. William Buchanan, and Samuel Purviance, Jr., and other principal inhabitants in Baltimore.

No. 16.

Friday, the 27th May, 1774.

And this day, at 10 o'clock, the honorable members of the late house of Burgesses, met by agreement, at the long room in the Raleigh tavern in this city, called the Apollo, when the following agreement was unanimously entered into by that patriotic assembly, in support of the constitutional liberties of America, against the late oppressive act of the British parliament, respecting the town of Boston, which, in the end, must affect all the colonies.

We, his majesty's most dutiful and loyal subjects, the late representatives of the good people of this country, having been deprived, by the sudden interposition of the executive part of this government, from giving our countrymen the advice we wished to convey to them, in a legislative capacity, find ourselves under the hard necessity of adopting this the only method we have left, of pointing out to our countrymen, such measures as in our opinion, are best fitted to secure our dearest rights and liberty from destruction, by the heavy hand of power, now lifted against North America. With much grief, we find that our dutiful applications to Great Britain, for security of our just, ancient, and constitutional rights, have not been only disregarded, but that a determined system is formed and pressed, for reducing the inhabitants of British America to slavery, by subjecting them to the payment of taxes, imposed without the consent of the people or their representatives, and that in pursuit of this system, we find an act of the British parliament, lately passed for stopping the harbor and commerce of the town of Boston, in our sister colony of Massachusetts bay, until the people there submit to the payment of such unconstitutional taxes, and which act most violently and arbitrarily deprives them of their property in wharfs erected by private persons, at their own great and proper expense, and which act is, in our opinion, a most dangerous attempt to destroy the constitutional liberty and rights of all North America.

It is farther our opinion, that as tea, on its importation into America, is charged with a duty imposed by parliament, for the purpose of raising a revenue, without the consent of the people, it ought not to be used by any person who wishes well to the constitutional rights and liberty of British America. And whereas, the India company have ungenerously attempted the ruin of America, by sending many ships loaded with tea, into the colonies, thereby intending to fix a precedent in favor of arbitrary taxation, we deem it highly proper, and do accordingly recommend it strongly to our countrymen, not to purchase or use any kind of East India commodity whatsoever, except saltpetre and spices, until the grievances of America are redressed. We are farther clearly of opinion, that an attack made on one of our sister colonies, to compel submission to arbitrary taxes, is an attack made upon all British America, and threatens ruin to the rights of all, unless the united wisdom of the whole be applied : and for this purpose, it is recommended to the committee of correspondence, that they communicate with their several corresponding committees, on the expediency of appointing deputies from the several colonies of British America, to meet in general congress, at such place annually as shall be thought most convenient, there to deliberate on those general measures, which the united interests of America may, from time to time require. A tender regard for the interests of our fellow subjects, the merchants and manufacturers of Great Britain, prevents us from going further at this time, most earnestly hoping that the constitutional principle of taxing the colonies without their consent, will not be persisted in, thereby to compel us, against our will, to avoid all commercial intercourse with Britain. Wishing them and our people free and happy, we are their affectionate friends, the late representatives of Virginia.

The above, was immediately signed by the speaker, and all the members of the late house of Burgesses, as well as by a number of clergymen, and other inhabitants of the colony, who, after having maturely considered the contents of the association, did most cordially approve and accede thereto.

No. 17.

At a general meeting of the freeholders, gentlemen, merchants, tradesmen, and other inhabitants of Baltimore county, held at the Court house of the said county, on Tuesday, May 31st, 1774.

CAPT. CHARLES RIDGELY, *Chairman.*

Resolved, 1st. That it is the opinion of this meeting, that the town of Boston is now suffering in the common cause of America, and that it is the duty of every colony in America to unite in the most effectual means to obtain a repeal of the late act of parliament, for blocking up the harbor of Boston. Dissentient three.

2d. That it is the opinion of this meeting, that if the colonies come into a joint resolution, to stop importations from, and exportations to Great Britain and the West Indies, until the act for blocking up the harbor of Boston be repealed, the same may be the means of preserving North America and her liberties. Dissentient three.

3d. That therefore the inhabitants of this county, will join in an association with the several counties of this province, and the principal colonies of America, to put a stop to the exports to Great Britain and the West Indies, after the first day of October next, or such other day as may be agreed on: and to put a stop to the imports from Great Britain, after the first day of December next, or such other day as may be agreed on, until the said act be repealed: and that such association shall be on oath. Dissentient nine.

4th. Unanimously, That it is the opinion of this meeting, that as the most effectual means of uniting all parts of this province, in such association as proposed, a general congress of deputies from each county be held at Annapolis, at such time as may be agreed on; and that if agreeable to the sense of our sister colonies, delegates shall be appointed from this province, to attend a general congress of delegates, from the other colonies, at such time and place as shall be agreed on, in order to settle and establish a general plan of conduct, for the important purposes aforementioned.

Resolved, 5th. Unanimously, that the inhabitants of this county will, and it is the opinion of this meeting, that the province ought to break off all trade and dealings with that colony, province, or town, which shall refuse or decline to come into similar resolutions, with a majority of the colonies.

6th. That Capt. Charles Ridgely, Charles Ridgely, son of John, Walter Tolley, Jr., Thomas Cockey Dye, William Lux, Robert Alexander, Samuel Purviance, Jr., John Moale, Andrew Buchanan, and George Risteau, be appointed a committee to attend a general meeting at Annapolis. And that the same gentlemen, together with John Smith, Thomas Harrison, William Buchanan, Benjamin Nicholson, Thomas Sollers, William Smith, James Gittings, Richard Moale, Jonathan Plowman, and William Spear, be a committee of correspondence, to receive and answer all letters, and on any emergency, to call a general meeting: and that any six of the number have power to act.

7th. That a copy of the proceedings be transmitted to the several counties of this province, directed to their committee of correspondence, and be also published in the Maryland Gazette, to evince to all the world, the sense they entertain of the invasion of their constitutional rights and liberties.

8th. That the chairman be desired to return the thanks of this meeting, to the gentlemen of the committee of correspondence from Annapolis, for their polite personal attendance, in consequence of an invitation by the committee of correspondence for Baltimore town.

Per order, WILLIAM LUX, *Clerk.*

No. 18.

Williamsburg, 31*st May*, 1774.

Gentlemen,—We had the honor of writing, the 28th inst., to the speaker of your assembly, enclosing him the resolutions of our late house of Burgesses, and a copy of the association entered into by the late representatives of Virginia, upon the dissolution of our assembly. We suppose, this letter with the other papers, must have got to hand, and that they have been communicated to you. We have now to acknowledge the receipt of your favor of the 25th, accompanying the several letters, &c., from Boston and Philadelphia. Our moderator, without loss of time, immediately convened as many of the late representatives as could be got together upon so short a notice, and we yesterday took this business under our most serious consideration. The result of our deliberations will best appear from the enclosed, to which we take the liberty of referring you, and beg that it may be immediately transmitted, through the hands of our friends in Philadelphia, to our friends in Boston, in the same manner as their sentiments and resolutions have been conveyed to us. We wish it had been in our power to have done any thing more decisive at present, but our situation would not admit of it, as you will readily judge, from the reasons suggested by our resolutions. We could wish to have known the sentiments of New York. We find a letter from the committee of correspondence in that province, mentioned in the Philadelphia letters, but no copy of it was enclosed, nor the purport of it mentioned. We shall hope to be favored, from time to time, with the sentiments and resolutions of all our sister colonies, and this, in the most expeditious manner.

We have the honor to be, gentlemen,

Your most obedient servants,

The Committee of Correspondence for Virginia.

To the committee of correspondence for Maryland.

At a meeting of twenty-five of the late representatives legally assembled by the moderator, it was agreed that letters be wrote to all our sister colonies, acknowledging the receipt of the letters and resolves from Boston, &c., informing them that before the same came to hand, the Virginia assembly had been unexpectedly dissolved, and most of the members returned to their respective counties. That it is the opinion of all the late house of Burgesses, who could be convened on the present occasion, that the colony of Virginia will concur with the other colonies, in such measures as shall be judged most effectual for the preservation of the common rights and liberty of British America; that they are of opinion particularly, that an association against importations will probably be entered into, as soon as the late representatives can be collected, and perhaps against exportations also, after a certain time. But that this must not be considered as an engagement on the part of this colony, which it would be presumption in us to enter into, and that we are sending despatches to call together the late representatives to meet at Williamsburg, on the first day of August next, to conclude finally, on those important questions.

Peyton Randolph, *Moderator.*

Ro. C. Nicholas,	George Washington,
Edmund Pendleton,	Francis Lightfoot Lee,
William Harwood,	Thomas Watson, Jr.
Richard Adams,	Robert Rutherford,
Thomas Whitling,	John Walker,
Henry Lee,	James Wood,
Samuel Liddick,	Thomas Blackburn,
Thomas Jefferson,	Wm. Langhorne,
Mann Page, Jr.	Edmund Berkely,
Charles Carter, (Lanc'r.)	Wm. Donelson,
James Mercer,	Paul Carrington,
R. Wormley Carter,	Lewis Burwell, (Gloster.)

No. 19.

At a general meeting of the merchants, traders, and other inhabitants of the borough of Norfolk, and town of Portsmouth, in the colony of Virginia, on Monday, the 30th of May, 1774,

It was resolved, That Thomas Newton, Jr., Esq., one of our late worthy burgesses, be appointed moderator of this meeting, and William Davies, clerk.

Mr. Newton accordingly took the chair, when the letters and other papers transmitted from Boston, Philadelphia and Baltimore, together with the resolution of the late house of Burgesses of this colony, and the association of the members and others after the dissolution of the general assembly, were severally read and heard, and upon the question put,

It was resolved, That Thomas Newton, Jr., Joseph Hutchings, John Goodrich, Paul Loyal, James Taylor,

Matthew Phrippe, Alexander Love, Robert Sheddon, Robert Taylor, Samuel Inglis, Samuel Ker, Henry Brown, John Greenwood, Niel Jamieson, John Mitchel, Alexander Skinner, William Harvey, Thomas Brown, Robert Gilmour, or any five of them, be a committee to correspond with the several committees of the different commercial towns on the continent, upon the important subject of those papers, and acquaint them with the sentiments of the inhabitants of these towns, and to take such other steps for the relief of our suffering brethren of Boston, and the establishment of the rights of the colonies, as to the committee shall appear most expedient and effectual.

WILLIAM DAVIES, *Clerk.*

No. 20.

Norfolk, May 31*st*, 1774.

Gentlemen,—The occasion is too serious to admit of apologies, for this unsolicited communication of our sentiments to you, at this alarming crisis to American freedom, for the time is come, the unhappy era is arrived, when the closest union among ourselves, and the firmest confidence in each other, are our only securities for those rights, which as men, and free men, we derive from nature and the constitution. The late hostile parliamentary invasion of the town of Boston, we deem an attack upon the liberties of us all. Of the particulars of that unhappy transaction, we presume you are already fully informed, and we doubt not, shudder with us at this systematic mode of depriving the unrepresented American of his rights and possessions, and vesting the crown with despotic power over the free born inhabitants of the capital of the Massachusetts bay. What measures are most proper to be adopted on this sad occasion, we are at a loss to point out; but we look to the wisdom of your city, in conjunction with the other large commercial towns on this continent, to take more immediately the lead in these important matters, and to fix upon such expedients in the regulation of trade, as may be most productive of relief to our suffering brethren of Boston, and the general establishment of the rights of these colonies; and you may rest assured, that in every measure conducive to this grand continental object, you will always meet with our most hearty concurrence. We are under great apprehensions for the people of Boston, lest they may sink under the weight of their misfortune; and at the same time, that we highly approve of the expediency of a congress, as proposed by several of the colonies, we think that the trading part of the community ought particularly to interfere, for nothing but the most speedy and efficacious measures can relieve them: and if after all, there should be found an unhappy necessity to reimburse the India company, for that just punishment they received, for their ungenerous attempts on our liberties, we trust there is no inhabitant of these colonies, who feels and thinks himself a freeman, but will cheerfully put his hand to his purse, and join in the general expense. Inclosed, we transmit to you the proceedings of the inhabitants of the borough of Norfolk and town of Portsmouth, together with letters and other papers from Boston, Philadelphia and Baltimore, as also copies of the resolutions, and other proceedings of the members of our late house of Burgesses, both before and after their dissolution. We hope to be able to inform you more particularly of the collected sense of the trade of this colony, at the general meeting of the merchants next week, at Williamsburg, when we expect farther despatches from the northward. We hope the favor of a free and full communication of your sentiments on this important occasion, and trust that your flourishing and respectable province, will still continue their generous endeavors for the establishment of the rights of the colonies, that the opposition of all America may be as extensive as the oppression. With the warmest attachment to the interests of the colonies, we are, gentlemen, most respectfully,

Your most obedient servants,

THOMAS NEWTON, Jr.	JOHN GREENWOOD,
JOSEPH L. HUTCHINGS,	ALEX. SKINNER,
PAUL LOYALL,	WM. HARVEY,
ALEX. LOVE,	NIEL JAMIESON.
SAMUEL INGLIS,	

To the committee of correspondence of Charleston, South Carolina.

No. 21.

Norfolk, June 2d, 1774.

Gentlemen,—We acknowledge the receipt of your interesting favor, and hope you will still continue to communicate your sentiments to us, on the important subject of your letter, in the freest and fullest manner. We are happy in so general a concurrence in opinion with you, and are ready to unite in any measures that may be generally thought for the advantage of the colonies, and the relief of our unhappy brethren of Boston. We sympathize most sincerely with them in their sufferings; our hearts are warmed with affection for them, and we trust they never will be deserted, nor left the solitary strugglers against arbitrary power. The act for blocking up their harbor, and stopping their trade, and the bill for altering and amending the charter of the colony of the Massachusetts bay, which Lord North has lately brought into the house of Commons, we view as fatal strokes to the liberties of these colonies, and a down right robbery of our rights; but we rest with a firm assurance that the paltry policy of attacking a town or a province singly, will never so unhappily delude us, as to disunite us from that joint, firm, and universal opposition of all British America, which, we trust, will always render abortive every such pernicious measure.

As we have had occasion to write to South Carolina, previous to this, our earliest opportunity of answering your favor, we transmit you a copy of that letter, which you will please to communicate as you may think it proper. You have also enclosed some other papers, from which you will be fully sensible that we are ready to unite in any measure for the public good.

We are, gentlemen, with great esteem,

Your obedient and most humble servants,

JOSEPH HUTCHINGS, PAUL LOYALL,
ALEX. SKINNER, WILLIAM HARVEY.
JAMES TAYLOR,

To the committee of Baltimore.

No. 22.

Baltimore, June 4th, 1774.

Gentlemen,—On the 25th ultimo, we received, (by express) from Philadelphia, a copy of your letter of the 13th, to the gentlemen of that city, and a copy of their reply thereto, together with the votes of your town meeting, on the truly alarming situation of your affairs, by the late act of parliament, for blocking up the harbor of Boston.

Could we remain a moment indifferent to your sufferings, the result of your noble and virtuous struggles in defence of American liberties, we should be unworthy to share in those blessings, which (under God,) we owe, in a great measure, to your perseverance and zeal in support of our common rights, that they have not ere now, been wrested from us, by the rapacious hand of power. Permit us, therefore, as brethren, fellow citizens and Americans, embarked in one common interest, most affectionately to sympathize with you, now suffering and persecuted in the common cause of our country, and to assure you of our readiness to concur in every reasonable measure that can be devised for obtaining the most effectual and speedy relief to our distressed friends.

Actuated by these sentiments, we immediately, on receipt of the letters aforesaid, called a meeting of the principal inhabitants, and appointed a committee of twelve persons, to correspond with you, the neighboring colonies, and particularly with the towns in this province, to collect the public sense of this important concern. We procured a general meeting of the freeholders and gentlemen of this county, the 31st ult., when the enclosed resolutions were agreed on, with a spirit and harmony, which, we flatter ourselves, prevails very generally through all parts of this province. The resolve of a general congress of deputies, in order to unite the sense of the whole colony on this interesting occasion, will, (we have reason to hope) be attended with success. Having addressed every county for that purpose, and the gentlemen of Annapolis concurring in the same design, as soon as the result of this congress is determined, we shall make you acquainted therewith.

In order to inspire the same zeal in others, with which we are actuated for your cause, we have transmitted copies of all the papers we received, to the gentlemen of Alexandria, Norfolk and Portsmouth, in Virginia, and have taken the liberty of recommending to our friends in Philadelphia, the necessity of setting a good example, as their influence would greatly preponderate in your favor. Although the gentlemen of Philadelphia have recommended a general congress, for proceeding by petition or remonstrance, we cannot see the least grounds of expecting relief by it. The contempt with which a similar petition was treated, in 1765, and many others since that period, convince us that policy or reasons of state, instead of justice and equity, are to prescribe the rule of our future conduct, and that something more sensible than supplications will best serve our purpose. The idea of a general congress, held forth by our resolves, as merely to unite such colonies as will associate in a general system of non-exportation and non-importation, both to be regulated in such degree and manner, as most suitable to the circumstances of each colony, and as to enable us (if necessary) to hold out longer without aggrieving one more than another.

Permit us, as friends, truly anxious for the preservation of your and our common liberties, to recommend firmness and moderation, under this severe trial of your patience, trusting that the supreme disposer of all events, will terminate the same, in a happy confirmation of American freedom. We are, with much sincerity,

Your truly sympathizing friends,

SAMUEL PURVIANCE, *Chairman.*

WM. BUCHANAN,

In behalf of the committee.

P. S. Your letter of the 13th May, with copy of your town vote, is just now come to hand.

To the committee of Boston.

No. 23.

Baltimore, June 4th, 1774.

Gentlemen,—We received by express, your letter of the 21st ult., covering the resolves of the town meeting of Boston, and copies of their very interesting letter to you, with your answer and resolve. A meeting of the town was immediately called, at which were present, a number of the most respectable inhabitants, before whom the letters and papers were read, who, viewing the act of parliament for shutting the port of Boston, as an arbitrary, cruel, and oppressive edict, infringing one of the fundamental principles of the constitution, by condemning unheard, and preceding any convictions of the supposed crime, immediately appointed a committee of twelve gentlemen, with instructions to them, to forward copies of the letters, &c., to the several counties of this province, and the neighboring colony of Virginia. And the better to collect the sense of the town and county of Baltimore, and to afford time for reflection on this very interesting and important subject, they appointed the 31st ult., for a general meeting, which was accordingly held on that day,—the resolutions of which, will best evince to the world their sentiments, on the measures now pursued by a corrupt, venal and arbitrary ministry, against the town of Boston, and through her against the liberties of this extensive continent. The alacrity and readiness, with which the gentlemen of your city have hitherto, with great spirit, entered into every measure that could promote the public good; the sacrifices they have made to private interests, to attain that end, and the happy effects resulting therefrom, convince us that Pennsylvania will unite in every prudent measure to preserve her liberties, and that of her American brethren. What those measures may be, we cannot determine. Our sentiments on the subject, we hold forth to the public, and nearly concurring with the gentlemen of Annapolis, (whose resolves were transmitted to you) we may venture to assert, nothing less favorable will be proposed by any county of this province, or adopted at the general meeting, which you will observe by our resolutions, is to be held at Annapolis. The idea we have formed of a general congress, as expressed in our fourth resolve, is by no means formed upon the opinion or necessity of such a congress, for the purpose of petitioning or remonstrating to the crown, or any branch of the legislature of Great Britain. The indignity offered by the ministry to every petition from America; the affected contempt with which they treated those transmitted in 1765, and every other since that time, leave us not the least ray of hope, that any application in that mode, would be productive of relief to the sufferings of Boston, whom we consider as a victim to ministerial vengeance, for wisely and justly opposing them, in their arbitrary attacks upon American liberty. We have proposed the congress to settle and establish a general plan of conduct for such colonies that may think fit to send deputies; their local circumstances and particular situation, may render some little diversity necessary, especially should the same influence, that has unhappily guided the councils of Great Britain, continue to prevail. We make no doubt, every effort will be used to enslave the colonies, and pave the way to enslave England itself. When such diversity is known, and a general system established, doubt and distrust among ourselves will be removed, confidence will take place, and our enemies both know and fear the power of American virtue, which they have most unjustly provoked. Should you think our resolves adequate to the measure, or that they may tend to inspire the gentlemen of your province with favorable sentiments to the general cause, we submit to you the propriety of their publication; and when your province has agreed on any plan, we shall be happy in having it communicated to us, together with your sentiments on our conduct. The discharge of our duty on this occasion, gives us great pleasure in affording the opportunity to express our sentiments of esteem for your public conduct, and respect to your private persons.

We are, gentlemen,

Your most obedient servants,

SAMUEL PURVIANCE, Jr.	THOMAS SOLLERS,
J. HARRISON,	JOHN MOALE,
ANDREW BUCHANAN,	WM. SPEAR,
ROBERT ALEXANDER,	WILLIAM LUX,
WM. BUCHANAN,	WILLIAM SMITH.
JONATHAN PLOWMAN,	

To the committee of Philadelphia.

No. 24.

At a meeting of a very considerable and respectable body of the inhabitants of Anne Arundel county, inclusive of those of the city of Annapolis, on Saturday, the 4th day of June, 1774:

Mr. Brice Thomas Beale Worthington, moderator.

1st. Resolved, unanimously, That it is the opinion of this meeting, that the town of Boston is now suffering in the common cause of America, and that it is incumbent on every colony in America, to unite in effectual means to obtain a repeal of the late act of parliament, for blocking up the harbor of Boston.

2d. Resolved, That it is the opinion of this meeting that if the colonies come into a joint resolution to stop all importations from, and exportations to Great Britain and the West Indies, till the said act be repealed, the same will be the most effectual means to obtain a repeal of the said act, and preserve North America and her liberties.

3d. Resolved, therefore, unanimously, That the inhabitants of this county, will join in an association, with the several counties in this province, and the principal colonies in America, to put a stop to exports to Great Britain and the West Indies, after the ninth day of October next, or such other day as may be agreed on; and to put a stop to the imports of goods not already ordered, and of those ordered that shall not be shipped from Great Britain, by the twentieth day of July next, or such other day as may be agreed on, until the said act shall be repealed; and that such association be on oath.

4th. Resolved, That as remittances can be made only from exports, after stopping the exports to Great Britain and the West Indies, it will be impossible for very many of the people of this province, who are possessed of valuable property, immediately to pay off their debts, and therefore, it is the opinion of this meeting, the gentlemen of the law ought to bring no suit for the recovery of any debt, due from any inhabitant of this province, to any inhabitant of Great Britain, until the said act be repealed, and further that they ought not to bring any suit for the recovery of any debt due to any inhabitant of this province, except in such cases where the debtor is guilty of a wilful delay in payment, having ability to pay, or is about to abscond, or remove his effects, or is wasting his substance, or shall refuse to settle his account.

5th. Resolved, That it is the opinion of this meeting that a congress of deputies from the several counties to be held at Annapolis, as soon as conveniently may be, will be the most speedy and effectual means of uniting all the parts of this province, in such association as proposed, and that if agreeable to the sense of our sister colonies, delegates ought to be appointed from this province, to attend a general congress of deputies, from the other colonies, at such time and place as may be agreed on, to effect unity in a wise and prudent plan, for the forementioned purpose.

6th. Resolved, unanimously, That the inhabitants of this county will, and it is the opinion of this meeting that the province ought, to break off all trade and dealings with that colony, province or town, which shall decline or refuse to come into similar resolutions of a majority of the colonies.

7th. Resolved, That Brice Thomas Beale Worthington, Charles Carroll, barrister, John Hall, William Paca, Samuel Chase, Thomas Johnson, Jr., Matthias Hammond, Thomas Sprigg, Samuel Chew, John Weems, Thomas Dorsey, Rezin Hammond and John Hood, Jr., be a committee to attend a general meeting at Annapolis, and of correspondence to receive and answer all letters, and on any emergency to call a general meeting, and that any six of the number have power to act.

Ordered, That a copy of these resolves be transmitted to the committees of the several counties of this province, and also published in the Maryland Gazette.

By order,

John Duckett,

Secretary of the Committee.

No. 25.

Annapolis, 5th June, 1774.

Gentlemen,—The Gazette was printed, and distributing before the resolutions of your county reached us. We enclose you those of this county, as well as copies of papers received yesterday from Virginia. We fear the Bostonians, whilst their brethren are deliberating, will lose all hope of an effectual union.

We are, gentlemen,
With the utmost regard,
Your most obedient servants,
The COMMITTEE of CORRESPONDENCE
for ANNE ARUNDEL COUNTY.

To the committee of correspondence for Baltimore county.

No. 26.

Baltimore, June 11th, 1774.

Dear Sir,—We transmitted you a copy of the resolutions entered into by the people of this county. Since which, similar resolves have been adopted, in several other counties, and a general congress of the whole province, is to be held the 22d inst. at Annapolis, to consider in an united manner, the case of our suffering brethren of Boston: all parts of this province discover the most forward zeal in the common cause,—and we sincerely wish Philadelphia was equally disposed to embark in the matter. The alarming strides with which parliament pushes their unfriendly designs, give a full confirmation to the fears we have often entertained of a settled determined plan of despotism being in view. We heartily pray for that union and harmony of sentiment, so essentially necessary to avert every insidious design against American liberties.

We are, dear sir,

Your friends and servants,

SAMUEL & ROBERT PURVIANCE.

To Jeremiah Lee, Esq., Boston.

No. 27.

Baltimore June 13*th*, 1774.

Gentlemen,—We took the liberty of addressing you on the 4th inst., with a copy of the resolves of this town and county, at a public meeting of the inhabitants, held the 31st ult. Since that time, most counties in this province, following the example of Annapolis and this place, have had public meetings, and entered into similar resolutions, all concurring in the same general sentiments of your sufferings in defence of our common rights, and expressing their cordial disposition to agree in the most effectual measures, for asserting and defending our constitutional liberties, and for procuring a repeal of the violent and arbitrary edict issued against the town of Boston. It affords us singular satisfaction to find the general sentiments of the good people of the province, and such in Virginia as we have corresponded with, so agreeable to our own apprehensions of this important cause, the cause of every American, and we sincerely congratulate you and every friend of our country, on that laudable zeal and patriotic spirit, which prevails among all ranks of our people, to assert and vindicate your cause. We have now the pleasure of giving you a recent proof of this by the enclosed copies of letters and resolves, which we received this day from the gentlemen of Norfolk and Portsmouth, in Virginia, which we judged of such importance to the common cause, that we now transmit copies thereof, by *express*, to the committee of Philadelphia, where a general meeting of the town and county is to be held, the day after to-morrow, hoping it may tend to inspire them with the same sentiments, so generally prevalent in the province.

A proposal has been made by some gentlemen of Chestertown, in this colony, to open a subscription for support of the poor inhabitants of your town, who may be most immediately distressed by the stagnation of business. Some of us have had the same object in contemplation, and determine to propose it to the general congress of deputies for the province, which, we doubt not, will be generally adopted. With the most affectionate wishes for your speedy and happy deliverance,

We are, gentlemen,

Your very humble servants,

Samuel Purviance, Jr, *Chairman*,

Wm. Buchanan,

In behalf of the committee.

To the committee of Boston.

No. 28.

Baltimore, 13*th June* 1774.

Gentlemen,—We did ourselves the pleasure of writing you, the 4th inst, per post, covering copy of the resolutions entered into at a general meeting of this county.

Having this day received from Norfolk in Virginia, a letter, enclosing copy of a letter to the gentlemen of Charleston in South Carolina, and also the resolutions of the town of Norfolk and Portsmouth, we now transmit you copies of the same by express, as we are informed there is to be a general meeting of your city, the 15th inst. When we consider the present important era, and the further design meditated against the freedom of America, it certainly ought to excite us to use every just endeavor to avert the impending ruin. We doubt not, every real friend to America, will take pleasure in the agreeable prospect of unanimity in the colonies, so absolutely necessary at the present time.

We are, gentlemen,

Your very humble servants,

SAMUEL PURVIANCE, Jr., *Chairman*,

In behalf of the committee.

To the committee of Philadelphia.

No. 29.

Boston, June 16*th*, 1774.

Gentlemen,—We last evening received your affectionate and generous letter of the 3d inst., enclosing your noble and spirited resolves. Nothing gives us a more animating confidence of the happy event of our present struggles for the liberties of America; or affords us greater support under the distresses we now feel, than the assurances we receive from our brethren, of their readiness to join with us in every salutary measure, for preserving the rights of the colonies, and of their tender sympathy for us, under our sufferings. We rejoice to find the respectable county of Baltimore so fully alarmed at the public danger, and so prudent and resolute in their measures to secure the blessings of freedom to their country. Our general assembly is now sitting at Salem, about twenty miles from this town. We expect that the members for a general congress will speedily be elected by them. We hope by the next opportunity, to send you a full account of their proceedings: the post just going off, we can only add, that we are, gentlemen, with the most unfeigned respect and esteem,

Your most humble servants,

By order of the Committee
of Correspondence,
WILLIAM COOPER, *Clerk.*

P. S. We think your caution of enclosing your letters to a friend is extremely just, at this crisis of our affairs, and we shall follow your example.

To Mr. Samuel Purviance, Jr., to be communicated to the committee of correspondence of Baltimore.

No. 30.

Baltimore, 17th June, 1774.

Gentlemen,—The want of opportunity has prevented us from advising you sooner, of the measures pursued, since we addressed you the 25th ult. The 31st May, a general meeting of our county was held at this place, when certain resolves (whereof you have copy enclosed,) were agreed on, and copies of the same transmitted to every county in the province, to Philadelphia, Boston, &c. Many of the other colonies following our example have already come into similar resolutions, and we have scarcely a doubt that all the rest will concur.

Your letter of the 2d inst., which we received a few days ago, by General Lee, affords the highest satisfaction in finding your sentiments on the Boston port bill, and other designs of administration, so correspondent with our own, and the general sense of those important subjects. Having learned that there was a general meeting of the city and county of Philadelphia, to be held last Wednesday, we immediately despatched an express, with copies of your letters and resolves, for that place and Boston, which we hope would prove of singular service in obviating some unfavorable impressions, made by the association of your late representatives, after the dissolution of your assembly, which were considered by many here, (and, we presume would by the people of Philadelphia,) far short of that spirit and zeal by which the gentlemen of your colony have ever been distinguished. As the association was agreed on before your late representatives had received the express from Philadelphia, or a perfect information on the subject, we are far from viewing their conduct in an unfavorable light. We have seen their reply to Philadelphia, by the express, which removes every suspicion of coolness or indifference.

Although the despotic intentions of administration, against the liberties of our country, are so manifest, "that he who runs may read them," without much reasoning on the subject. If not wilfully blind to our own interests, we must be convinced that on union and harmony amongst ourselves, (under God) our salvation from slavery perpetual to us and our posterity must we depend, unless we determine tamely to surrender all our rights at once to the will of a rapacious profligate ministry, who have nearly subdued the struggles for liberty in Britain, and with a conquest of American liberties, bid fair to demolish the whole British constitution. However alarming the Boston port bill may be in its nature and tendency, what is it compared to the effects of the two other bills, for altering and changing the constitution of their government, and for the trial of persons concerned in shedding the blood of our fellow subjects, who may be removed elsewhere, or even to England for trial, as if intended to protect them from the justice of the laws. If we can tamely submit to these things, what security remains for life, liberty or property.

A general meeting of delegates, from every county in this province, will be held, as soon as we can know the resolutions of your province, Pennsylvania and New York, by whose conduct we imagine the other colonies will chiefly be determined in their conduct.

We have, at present, every reason to hope for the greatest harmony of sentiment in the good people of this province, who discover a truly laudable spirit and readiness to concur, in whatever measures are thought best to adopt, either of a total or partial non-importation and non-exportation. We shall not fail to embrace every opportunity of advising you whatever new may occur to us, on these or any other public concerns, and shall hope for a friendly communication of your sentiments. Being, with much respect,

Your most obedient servants,

Samuel Purviance, Jr.
Robert Alexander,
John Smith
Wm. Buchanan.
Wm. Spear,
Andrew Buchanan
Wm. Lux.

Enclosed, is a Philadelphia paper, just come to hand.

To the Committee of Correspondence at Norfolk and Portsmouth.

Per Negro Cesar, in Mr. Goodrich's boat.

No. 31.

Frederick Town, 20th June, 1774.

Gentlemen,—Your letter of the 1st current, to the representatives of this county, was produced at our meeting, and we think it necessary to return you thanks, for acquainting us so early of your resolutions. You will find by ours, (which will be published in the next Maryland Gazette) how far we agree with you in the mode proposed for obtaining a repeal of the late acts of parliament, so subversive of the liberties of America. It will always give us pleasure to receive any intelligence from you, relative to the redress of our grievances. We are, with great respect, gentlemen,

Your very humble servants,

GEO. SCOTT, BENJ. DULANEY,
ARCH'D BOYD, THOMAS SCHLEY,
JOHN CARY, CONRAD GROSH,
CHRS'TN EDELEN, PETER HOFFMAN.
JOHN HANSON, Jr.

To Messrs. William Lux, Robert Alexander, James Gittings, Andrew Buchanan, William Spear, William Buchanan, and Samuel Purviance, Jr., gentlemen of the Committee of Correspondence for Baltimore county.

No. 32.

Votes and proceedings of the town of Boston, June 17th, 1774.

At a legal and very full meeting of the freeholders and other inhabitants of the town of Boston, by adjournment, at Faneuil hall, June, 17, 1774:

The Hon. John Adams, Esq., *Moderator.*

Upon a motion made, the town again entered into the consideration of that article in the warrant, viz. "to consider and determine what measures are proper to be taken upon the present exigency of our public affairs, more especially, relative to the late edict of a British Parliament, for blocking up the harbor of Boston, and annihilating the trade of this town," and after very serious debates thereon,

Voted, (with only one dissentient) that the committee of correspondence be enjoined forthwith, to write to all the other colonies, acquainting them that we are not idle, that we are deliberating upon the steps to be taken on the present exigencies of our public affairs; that our brethren, the landed interests of this province, with an unexampled spirit and unanimity, are entering into a non-consumption agreement; and that we are waiting with anxious expectation, for the result of a continental congress, whose meeting we impatiently desire, in whose wisdom and firmness, we can confide, and in whose determinations, we shall cheerfully acquiesce.

Agreeably to order, the committee of correspondence laid before the town such letters, as they had received, in answer to the circular letters, wrote by them to the several colonies, and also the sea port towns in this province, since the reception of the Boston port bill; and the same being publicly read.

Voted, unanimously, That our warmest thanks be transmitted to our brethren on the continent, for the humanity, sympathy and affection, with which they have been inspired, and which they have expressed towards this distressed town, at this important season.

Voted, unanimously, That the thanks of this town be, and hereby are given to the committee of correspondence, for their faithfulness in the discharge of their trust, and that they be desired to continue their vigilance and activity in that service.

Whereas, the overseers of the poor, in the town of Boston, are a body politic by law, constituted for the reception and distribution of all charitable donations, for the use of the poor of said town:

Voted, That all grants and donations to this town, and the poor thereof, at this distressing season, be paid and delivered into the hands of said overseers, and by them appropriated and distributed in concert with the committee lately appointed by this town, for the consideration of ways and means of employing the poor.

Voted, That the town clerk be directed to publish the proceedings of this meeting, in the several newspapers.

The meeting was then adjourned to Monday, the 27th of June, instant.

Attest,

WILLIAM COOPER, *Town Clerk.*

Boston, June 20th, 1774, 1 *o'clock, P. M.*

Gentlemen,—The foregoing votes and proceedings of this town, are just received from the press; we have only time to inform you, that our general assembly have appointed five gentlemen, to meet at a congress, at Philadelphia or elsewhere, on the first of September next, upon which the house was dissolved; for further particulars, must refer you to our next, as the post is now waiting.

In behalf of the Committee of Correspondence,

Gentlemen,

Your humble servant,

NATHANIEL APPLETON, *Chairman.*

To Mr. Samuel Purviance, merchant in Baltimore, Maryland.

No. 33.

Philadelphia, June 24th, 1774.

Gentlemen,—Time only admits the forwarding the resolves passed on Saturday, at a large and respectable meeting of the freeholders of this city and county.

Yesterday, our committee met, in order to prosecute the great and important business entrusted to them, which they have so much at heart.

Our counties are in motion, Lancaster and Chester have met. From the rest we have not yet heard.

Our subscription will be opened this week. The committee have adjourned till to-morrow, to deliberate and determine on what is committed to them by the 4th resolve.

I am to inform you, it is the desire of the committee, "that all letters for them, be directed under cover, to Charles Thomson, *at or near* Philadelphia."

Please to communicate this to the committee at Annapolis.

I am gentlemen,

Your humble servant,

CHARLES THOMSON.

Mr. Samuel Purviance and others, Committee at Baltimore.

No. 34.

Boston, 23d June, 1774.

Gentlemen,—Your favor of the 3d inst., now lies before the committee. We cannot but gratefully receive the generous sympathy and tender concern of our distant brethren for the distresses of the town of Boston, and esteem ourselves particularly obliged to the benevolent town of Chester, for their early interposition and tenders of benevolence, towards the afflicted poor of this devoted metropolis.

You conceive with justice, that we are suffering in the common cause; but being supported in the conflict with such liberal and seasonable aids, we presume, by the blessing of heaven, that this severe trial of the fortitude of the citizens, will never terminate in the surrender of the liberties of America.

The port bill, execrable as it is, and unparalleled for its severity, is executed infinitely beyond the rigor of the letter; a discretionary power to accumulate distress, is evidently betrusted to the executioner of the law;

—but you may rest assured, gentlemen, that we find greater difficulties in repressing the indignation of the people, than in inspiring them with a proper degree of spirit, fortified by the kind assurance of the countenance and assistance of the other colonies, though they bleed at every vein, they will never desert the common interest. Much we have to sacrifice, should the present measures be protracted, but in a cause so important, what sacrifice can be too great?

We cannot but applaud the spirit and determined virtue of the town of Chester, in their public transactions. A happy concurrence of sentiment and exertion, throughout the continent, at this interesting period, bodes well to the liberties of America. May this darling object forever attract our attention, and success crown the general struggle.

We shall not fail to communicate such interesting matters, as may be worthy your attention. The smiles and blessings of numerous poor, await your purposed relief. Please to consign whatever you may think proper to contribute to their necessities, to John Barrett, Esq., merchant in Boston, who is authorized to dispense your bounty. We shall esteem ourselves honored by your communications, and are, gentlemen, with much esteem,

Your most obedient humble servants,

Samuel Adams,
Benjamin Church, Jr.
John Sweetser, Jr.

By order of the Committee, for the town of Boston.

P. S. To increase the embarrassments of the town of Boston, our provision vessels, which are directed by the act to take a permit at Marblehead, before they are suffered to enter this harbor, are now compelled to unlade there, in pretence of preventing the conveyance of unadmissable goods;—but in fact, as some of their own officers have declared, to accumulate new distresses on this unhappy town.

SAMUEL ADAMS, *Chairman.*

To the Committee of Correspondence of Chester.

No. 35.

Annapolis, 26*th June*, 1774.

Gentlemen,—The enclosed resolutions, which we are directed to communicate, contain the sense of this province of a union, and general plan of conduct in defence of the liberties of America, in the present dangerous and truly alarming crisis. We feel ourselves happy, in the firm and steady spirit which animates the people of this province, to pursue those means which they judge the most speedy and effectual to prevent the fall of Boston, and the Massachusetts government; and by such prevention, to save America from destruction. It is our most fervent wish and sanguine hope, that your colony has the same disposition and spirit, and that, by a general congress, such a plan may be struck out, as may effectually accomplish the grand object in view. We are also directed to propose, that the general congress be held at the city of Philadelphia, the twentieth of September next. The limits of our province, and the number of its inhabitants, compared with yours, afforded an opportunity of collecting our general sense, before the sentiments of your colony could be regularly ascertained, and therefore, as this province had the first opportunity, it has taken the liberty of making the first proposition.

We request that you will forward our resolutions and proposition, to the colonies southward of you. If any circumstance unknown to us, should render the time or place inconvenient to your colony, you will oblige us by advising us of it, as soon as possible, and mentioning a time and place more agreeable. We shall be thankful for a speedy communication of every thing you may think of consequence.

We are, gentlemen,
With the utmost respect,
Your most obedient servants.

Signed by the DEPUTIES FROM MARYLAND.

To the Committee of Correspondence for Virginia.

No. 36.

Annapolis, 27th June, 1774.

Gentlemen,—We have sent you our letters for Pennsylvania, which enclose those for New Jersey, Rhode Island, New Hampshire, New York, Connecticut, Massachusetts, and the three lower counties, and request you will immediately despatch an express to Philadelphia. We are about closing up our letters for the southward, and we have sent a duplicate of our letter for South Carolina, which contains one to Georgia, for Mr. Purviance to send by the second express to Philadelphia, that some friend of his may take the chance of an early opportunity. We shall, as soon as we can get copies, send Mr. Purviance duplicates of our letters to the three lower counties.

We are, gentlemen.

Your most obedient servants,

TH. JOHNSON, JR.
WM. PACA,
SAMUEL CHASE.

We have enclosed, for the three lower counties.

To any of the gentlemen of the Committee of Correspondence, for Baltimore county.

No. 37.

Charles Town, South Carolina,
July 8th, 1774.

Gentlemen,—I am ordered by the most numerous meeting of the inhabitants of this colony, that was ever convened together, since our unhappy differences with the mother country, to transmit you a copy of their resolutions, under the fullest persuasion that you will readily concur in every necessary measure that can be fallen upon for restoring to British America, her just rights and liberties.

I am, gentlemen,

Your most humble servant,

G. G. POWELL, *Chairman.*

To the Committee of Correspondence, for the colony of Maryland, at Baltimore.

No. 38.

Boston, July 16th, 1774.

Gentlemen,—Your important letter of the 27th ult., with the enclosures, came safe to hand, and were regarded as "good news from a far country." The part taken by the province of Maryland, must henceforth stop the mouths of those blasphemers of humanity, who have affected to question the existence of public virtue. So bright an example as you have set, cannot fail to animate and encourage even the lukewarm and indifferent, more especially such honest men as wish to be assured of support, before they engage in so weighty an enterprise. The account you give us, of the spirit and magnanimity of the people of Virginia, confirms us in the opinion we have ever had of that ancient colony, of whose disinterested virtue this province has had ample experience. The noble sacrifice you stand ready to make of the staple commodity of your province, so materially affecting the revenue of Great Britain, and your generous interposition in our favor, have our warmest acknowledgments. So much honor, wisdom, public and private virtue, so much readiness in every colony to afford every species of aid and assistance, that the suffering state requires, must convince the venal herd, that notwithstanding they may be utterly unacquainted with the meaning of the word patriotism, it has, however, a substantial existence in North America.

With the smiles of all governing providence, upon the vigorous efforts of our inestimable brethren at home and abroad, we promise ourselves a final deliverance from the calamities we are now subjected to, and which for our own, our country, and posterity's political salvation, we resolve, by God's assistance, to sustain with fortitude and patience. We are, gentlemen, your friends and fellow countrymen,

Signed per order,

WILLIAM COOPER, *Clerk.*

To Samuel Purviance and others, of the Committee of Correspondence at Baltimore.

No. 39.

Philadelphia, July 25th, 1774.

Gentlemen,—As Messrs. Dickinson and Read are both out of town, I am directed to inform you, that our assembly met last week, and appointed deputies to attend the congress.

I have likewise the honor to enclose you the resolves and instructions drawn up by the provincial committee, by which you will see the sense of this province.

I am, gentlemen,

Your humble servant,

CHARLES THOMSON.

To Mr. Samuel Purviance, for the Committee at Baltimore.

No. 40.

Norfolk, August 3d, 1774.

Gentlemen,—I am directed by the committee of correspondence to transmit you the enclosed association and instructions, the result of a week's most studious deliberation at Williamsburg. The delegates appointed and instructed by almost every county in this extensive colony, met in convention, with a great variety of different opinions with respect to the mode of redress, although all agreed as to the oppressive and dangerous right claimed by parliament, of taxing and punishing us at their arbitrary pleasure. They all united, however, in the enclosed association, which is subscribed and adopted by the good people of this colony, with that readiness that manifests the zeal of the planters in the cause, for upon them we chiefly depend with respect to the stoppage of tobacco. The merchants that are natives are unanimous on this, and of those that are not, all that are married and fixed among us are enemies to the power claimed by parliament of taxing us, and we doubt not will act agreeably to the general association of this colony, and the measures that may be adopted by the congress. We hope the conditional non-exportation agreement adopted by us will prove agreeable to the patriotic gentlemen of your province, as we have reason to believe a non-importation agreement will prove effectual. It was thought better to hang out the other *in terrorem*, and after our planters had made what profit they could of the crops they had raised, that they might be encouraged to turn their force to some other article of produce, and deprive the exchequer of that immense revenue it received from that article. The several counties in this colony are liberally contributing to the relief and support of the people of Boston, who are esteemed worthy sufferers in this grand cause of all America. As to North Carolina, I am informed by a gentleman of veracity, just arrived from

Bute county in that province, that expresses had been despatched through all the colony, desiring each county to send two delegates to a convention to be held at Johnson court house, which they thought was the most central place in the province. There seems to be a greater spirit of unanimity on this occasion than on any other that ever engrossed the thoughts of the people of this colony, and we hope the whole continent will be as one man in this glorious opposition.

I have the honor to be, gentlemen,

Your most ob't humble serv't,

WILLIAM DAVIES.

To Samuel Purviance and others, committee at Baltimore.

No. 41.

Williamsburg, August 4, 1774.

Gentlemen,—Delegates from the different counties in this colony composed of the representatives of this people, met in this city on Monday last, to consider and deliberate on the present critical and alarming situation of the British American colonies.

As these matters are still the subjects of their deliberation, we cannot at present make you so fully acquainted with their determinations as we could wish. The expediency and necessity, however, of a general congress of deputies from the different colonies was so obvious, that the meeting have already come to the resolutions respecting it, which we now take the liberty to inclose you, and of which they have directed us to give you the earliest intelligence.

We request the favor of you to forward our letter to Philadelphia, and are with great respect, gentlemen,

Your most obedient humble servants,

PEYTON RANDOLPH,
ROBERT C. NICHOLAS,
DUDLEY DIGGES.

To the Committee of Correspondence of Maryland.

Virginia, Monday the first day of August, in the year of our Lord one thousand seven hundred and seventy-four.

At a general meeting of delegates from the different counties in this colony convened in the city of Williamsburg, to take under their consideration the present critical and alarming situation of the continent of North America:

The Honorable Peyton Randolph, Esq. in the chair.

The moderator recommended it to the meeting to proceed with that prudence, decency and order which the importance of the several matters that would come under their consideration required, and laid before them sundry letters and papers received by the committee of correspondence from the different colonies, which being read,

It was unanimously resolved, that it is the opinion of this meeting that it will be highly conducive to the security and happiness of the British Empire, that a general congress of deputies from all the colonies assemble, as quickly as the nature of their situations will admit, to consider of the most proper and effectual manner of so operating on the commercial connexion of the colonies with the mother country, as to procure redress for the much injured province of Massachusetts Bay; to secure British America from the ravage and ruin of arbitrary taxes, and speedily as possible to procure the return of that harmony and union so beneficial to the whole empire, and so ardently desired by all British America.

And then the meeting adjourned till to-morrow morning, nine o'clock.

Tuesday, August 2, 1774.

The delegates having met according to adjournment, resumed the consideration of the several important matters laid before them, and having spent the day therein, postponed the further consideration and discussion thereof till to-morrow. And then the meeting adjourned till to-morrow, nine o'clock.

Resolved, That the honorable Peyton Randolph, Esq., Richard Henry Lee, George Washington, Patrick Henry, Richard Bland, Benjamin Harrison, and Edmund Pendleton, Esqs. be appointed deputies on the part of this colony, to meet the deputies appointed or to be appointed by the other colonies in general congress, and that they do repair to the city of Philadelphia, on Monday the fifth of next month, for the purposes aforesaid.

No. 42.

Baltimore, August 4, 1774.

Gentlemen,—By order of the committee of correspondence for this town, we have shipped on board the sloop America, Perkins Allen, master, 3000 bushels of corn, 20 barrels of rye flour, 2 barrels of pork, and 21 barrels of bread, for the relief of our brethren, the distressed inhabitants of your town, being in virtue of subscriptions raised by the inhabitants of Baltimore town on that account. In the bill of lading for said articles, are also included 1000 bushels of corn, which we have purchased and shipped for the same account, on the strength of a subscription now making by the inhabitants of Annapolis, which a gentleman of their committee has assured us should be paid to us when their collection is made. As there was spare room in the vessel we were glad of an opportunity of forwarding to you a part of their benevolent intentions. We flatter ourselves the good people of this province, who have in general discovered a hearty disposition to sympathize in your grievances, will generously contribute according to their abilities, to maintain and support every sufferer in your and their own common cause. If we can be the least instrumental in furthering any contributions made in favor of your inhabitants, it will give us the most sincere pleasure, and some opportunity of exercising the grateful sense of many obligations which, as individuals, we are under, to many good people of your province.

We are with the highest respect, gentlemen,

Your most humble servants,

SAMUEL and ROBERT PURVIANCE.

To the Committee of Correspondence for the town of Boston.

No. 43.

Williamsburg, August 5, 1774.

Sir,—As the resolves of all the colonies which had come to hand in this meeting, adopted your appointment of Philadelphia as the place to hold the congress in; as the first of September or thereabouts hath been fixed upon by all of them (except your province) as a fit time; and as the time is now so near at hand as to render it difficult, if practicable, to change it, without putting too much to the hazard; it was resolved here to abide by the general choice of Philadelphia, though judged an improper place, and to fix upon the 5th of September, (as the South Carolinians have done) for the time.

Those measures or appointments wore more the effects of a seeming necessity than choice; and entered into by us to prevent any disappointment or confusion which might arise from a change of them, being finally agreed to, after Lancaster and the 15th of September, were the time and place first chosen.

For the resolutions of, and proceedings in our meeting, I refer you to the letter wrote by our committee of correspondence to that of yours. We never before had so full a meeting of delegates at any one time, as upon the present occasion. I shall not add, being a good deal hurried, but with esteem remain, sir,

Your most ob't humble servant,

GEO. WASHINGTON.

To Thos. Johnson, Jr. Esq., Annapolis.

No. 44.

Annapolis, August 10, 1774.

Sir,—The inclosed copies will show you the proceedings in Virginia. The letter from Col. Washington to Mr. Johnson, you will perceive, was not designed for public view. We are sorry that the meeting is to be so early as the 5th of September, but perhaps it will be better then, and at Philadelphia, than to run the risk of a new appointment.

The letter to Mr. Thompson, we suppose, contains duplicates of what was sent to us, and we imagine the pass will be a sufficient conveyance, without sending an express. Mr. Paca is not in town, but our letter contains a concurrence to the time and place.

We are, sir, your most ob't servants,

Thos. Johnson, Jr.
Samuel Chase.

To Samuel Purviance, Esq. chairman of the committee of correspondence, Baltimore.

No. 45.

Baltimore, Sept, 28*th,* 1774.

Gentlemen,—We have received information of 30 chests of tea being shipped on board a ship chartered by Messrs. William Kelly & Co. of London, and bound for this province, and on enquiry we have learnt that a ship called the Generous Friends, Capt. Nailor, sailed from London the latter end of July, with goods on board from that house, bound to Maryland. We therefore give you the earliest notice, that you may be prepared how to act on the occasion. We are of opinion that if the entry at the custom house can be prevented, and the tea sent back, it would be the best mode of proceeding, but this we submit to your better judgment, not doubting that you will pursue such measures as will best contribute to preserve the liberties of America.

We are very respectfully, gentlemen,

Your friends and servants,

Samuel Purviance, Jr.

William Lux,

In behalf of the committee.

To the committees of Chester and Annapolis.

No. 46.

Oxford, October 20th, 1774.

Gentlemen,—We are appointed by the committees of Talbot and Dorchester counties to address to your care some corn and rye collected for the support of the suffering poor of Boston. Our being disappointed in sending it by a ready conveyance from our place, has occasioned our ordering it to your care; especially as we have been well advised Mr. Purviance has been kind enough to offer storage and assistance in those cases. Should he have any vessel to accept the freight we would be glad, otherwise we understand Mr. Mark Alexander has offered to have it sent to them. By some of these conveyances we hope it will be as speedily conveyed as possible; and as to the freight, we must rely on your having it on as good terms as you can, and the amount shall either be transmitted to Baltimore for the person undertaking to carry, or paid by the order of your committee here, to whomsoever it shall be directed.

We are, gentlemen, with great esteem,

Your very humble servants,

James Murray,

Charles Crookshanks.

To the gentlemen of the Committee of Baltimore county.

No. 47.

Harford County, December, 1774.

Gentlemen,—Mr. Joseph McGoffin, has lately sold a cask of tea, to Mr. William Young of Harford town, and given a certificate under his hand, that the same had never paid any duty whatever. It was likewise attested, that he was a man of exceeding good character; upon which the committee of this county were of opinion, that Mr. Young might be permitted to vend the same, as being consistent with the resolves of the continental congress.

A quarter chest of tea, sold by the same gentleman, to Mr. Robert Tremble, has been carried to Joppa, and there seized by order of the committee, who have had Mr. Tremble up before them, and he informs them that he does not know whether a duty has been paid or not on it, but is to give further information and satisfaction on the subject, at a future day.

As we cannot search so deeply into this affair, without your assistance, the merchant being in your jurisdiction; should be glad you would enquire into the affair, and give us such light into it, as you can come at, that the public may be served agreeable to the trust reposed in us.

We are, gentlemen,

Your most humble servants,

Jo. Mathews,	Wm. Smithson,
Aquila Hall,	John Taylor,
Benjamin Rumsey,	George Bradford,
Wm. Webb,	Thos. Johnson.

To the gentlemen of the Committee of Baltimore county.

December 7th, 1774, answered, and a certificate enclosed.

Attest,

John Boyd, *Clerk.*

No. 48.

Frederick Town, 21*st October*, 1774.

Gentlemen,—As we have every day different accounts of your proceedings relative to teas, which have been lately imported, we think it necessary to apply to you for information, that we may know how to act with regard to the tea brought to this place. We have lately taken away from a Mr. Ferguson of this place, a chest of tea weighing 360 gross, and have stored it till he produces a certificate of its not having paid duty. Indeed it has been proposed at our last meeting, to store every pound of tea in the possession of the merchants, effectually to prevent every possibility of dutied tea from being sold amongst us. And that measure is only delayed till we hear from you, whether you would advise it, or what more effectual method you have fallen on to prevent the mischief.

We are, gentlemen,

Your very humble servants,

Signed per order of the Committee,

ARCHIBALD BOYD, *Clerk.*

To the gentlemen of the Committee of Correspondence for Baltimore county, Baltimore town.

Baltimore, May 24th, 1774.

To the gentlemen of Norfolk and Portsmouth,—On Tuesday last, we received by express from a committee of correspondence, lately appointed at Philadelphia a number of papers, whereof we take the liberty of enclosing you copies, in order to give you the earliest advice in a matter wherein we conceive we not only on our own, but yours and the general interest of every American, is most seriously concerned, by the late severe parliamentary edict, issued against the town of Boston, a measure so violent, that we presume no man who values liberty or property can, with indifference, behold a sister colony so cruelly treated for their spirited zeal in the common cause of American rights.

On the receipt of the papers referred, a meeting of the inhabitants of this town was immediately called, and the papers read to them, in order to collect the general sense, as well as we could, in so little time, what measures we ought to take. A committee of 12 persons were chosen, whereof you have the names annexed, in order to correspond with such committees as may be appointed in any part of our own, or the neighboring colonies, and to endeavor by every reasonable means in our power, to promote in a peaceable, decent, and regular manner, such measures as may be judged most expedient to obtain relief for our brethren of Boston, now suffering for the common cause of America. Though we understand the gentlemen of Philadelphia have ordered the express, as far as Williamsburg, with copies of these papers, yet we think it a matter of the highest importance, that all the commercial towns should harmonise in sentiments on so important an occasion, and therefore doubt not your accepting, in a favorable manner, this early communication of our intentions.

It has been proposed to collect, as early as possible, the general opinion whether we ought not to apply to the governor to convene the assembly, which, if judged best, we hope may be granted, if his hands are not tied up by ministerial mandates. In the meantime, we have written to the gentlemen at Annapolis, to take their sense of such a measure.

We flatter ourselves with great hopes from the well known spirit and zeal of the gentlemen of your province, one of the most ancient, extensive and prosperous in America, and hitherto foremost in the assertion of American rights, that they will not desert the cause of a province and town, famed like themselves, for a generous regard to the rights of their fellow subjects.

If we can but for a moment, only consider the dangerous tendency of the Boston port bill, as it may affect the commercial towns on this extensive continent, and the dreadful power with which it invests the crown, of immediately annihilating millions of property, vested in wharves and stores, we cannot but tremble for a measure, which, if enforced against any one town may, and most certainly will be, extended to all.

We shall take the liberty to advise you, if any thing new yet may occur on this subject, and shall at all times be glad to know your sentiments on this, or any other similar matter.

We are, with the greatest respect,

Gentlemen,

Your most humble servants.

Signed in behalf of the Committee,

SAMUEL PURVIANCE, Jr.
JOHN SMITH,
WM. BUCHANAN,
JOHN MOALE,
WM. SMITH.

To Dr. James Taylor, Messrs. Matthew Phrip, John Goodrich, Thomas Newton, Jr., and all others, the principal gentlemen of Norfolk and Portsmouth.

London, 12*th April*, 1775.

To the General Committee of Correspondence of Baltimore, in Maryland,—Sir, the committee of West India planters and merchants of the city of London, having applied to us to dispose in the province of Maryland of some copies of the evidence produced by them, at the bar of the house of Commons; we, at their desire, and in their name, do request your acceptance of the enclosed pamphlet.

We are, with the greatest respect, sir,

Your most obedient humble servants,

WM. & R. MOLLESON.

To the Chairman of the Committee of Baltimore county, Maryland.

Annapolis, March 26th, 1775.

Gentlemen,—Your letter of the 23d inst. we received yesterday, and we take this opportunity of thanking you for the communication of the extracts of the proceedings of your committee. These extracts shall be sent early to-morrow to the press, and we doubt not, of their being inserted in the next Maryland Gazette. We agree with you in opinion, that it may promote the public cause, if the committee of each county pass a vote of approving the conduct of the New York Committee. We shall use our endeavors to obtain a vote to that effect, at the next meeting of the committee for this county. At this critical juncture, a firm union of the colonies, and a rigid adherence to the continental association, we deem, under God, the most effectual means of preserving our liberties; every means, therefore, of tending to disunite the colonies, and to sow groundless jealousies between them, ought to be strictly guarded against. Invidious calumnies have been diligently propagated by the enemies of American liberty, to create distrust, to blind the people, and to seduce them from a steady pursuit of their true interests. Happily, such execrable designs have hitherto failed, and a speedy detection of the lie of the day, has served only to confound and stigmatize the secret contrivers and abettors of those transitory falsehoods; to men of that stamp, public infamy is no punishment; the greatest they can suffer, arises from the failure of their schemes; and built on fallacy and deception, they must ever fail. But there are other practices more dangerous to American rights, than those just mentioned, because they may originate from, at least, receive the sanction of men in public stations of the highest trust. The administration of justice may be made subservient to state policy, and gentlemen of unexceptionable character, of independent spirit and firmness, may be removed from office, to make room for persons of more compliant temper, and of more courtly principles.

We are, gentlemen, with due regard,

Your most obedient and humble servants,

CHARLES CARROLL, THOMAS JOHNSON, Jr.
CHARLES CARROLL of Carrollton,
J. HALL, SAMUEL CHASE.

To the Committee of Baltimore county.

Baltimore, July 21*st*, 1775.

Gentlemen,—In the month of December last, you were kind enough to permit my landing a quantity of mdze. from on board the Snow Potomac, which mdze. still remains in store, under your direction, and I would beg leave to remark, that I do not deem it safe in its present situation, as it is exposed to the mercy of any king's cruiser, that may be ordered this way. Yesterday's post brought me a letter from one of the proprietors, requesting I would, with your permission, remove a part of it to the head of Elk, there to be stored till the times were more favorable for the disposal thereof. I request your indulgence in this matter, under such restrictions as you may deem reasonable, and also, that you will be pleased to allow me to distribute remainder in such parts of the town as you may deem most eligible for its safety; the sooner you take this matter into consideration the better, for every day increases the danger it is subject to.

I am, very respectfully,

Gentlemen,

Your obedient servant,

DAVID STEWART.

Committee for Baltimore county.

Alexandria, June 25th, 1775.

Gentlemen,—Your obliging favor was handed to us very early this morning, by Capt. Hendrick, and holding the measure recommended by you to be highly necessary and expedient, we repaired to the office, examined the mail, and found such a packet as you mention. The contents were examined, and did not prove very important; consisting of sundry copies of Gen. Burgoyne's speech; the act for restraining the trade of the colonies, and two letters from Lord Dartmouth, confirming only the report of the high and absolute power vested in his majesty's general officers in the American service. The powers are not defined, but to us it appears they have a right to do as they please with us.

We are, gentlemen,

With great esteem and regard,

Your most obedient servants,

JOHN DALTON, JAMES HENDRICKS,
ROBERT H. HARRISON, JOHN MUIR.
GEORGE GILPIN,

To Samuel Purviance, Robert Alexander, and John Boyd, Esqrs., in Baltimore.

In Provincial Convention,
Annapolis, 4th August, 1775.

Resolved, That this convention will replace any arms, or powder, or lead, that may be delivered to the order of Messrs. Samuel Purviance, William Smith, and David Stewart, or any two of them, by the people of Bermuda, or will pay the just and full value thereof at farthest, as soon as America shall be in a settled state.

G. DUVALL, *Clerk.*

No. 49.

Philadelphia, January 29, 1776.

Dear Sir,—I received your favor of the 20th, informing me of Mr. Lux's resignation. The marine committee met the next day after your letter got here, a majority of whom were of opinion that a letter should be wrote to Mr. Lux, to request him to act in his appointment, and Mr. Morris was requested to write in behalf of the committee to him on that subject; they were also of opinion, in case Mr. Lux should refuse, that the business should go on under the direction of yourself, Mr. Chase and Mr. Stewart. I should have been very glad to have had your brother put on that service in Mr. Lux's room, but the committee in general thought it unnecessary to add another, seeing two good men had agreed to join Mr. Chase in the service; as Mr. Chase is entirely unacquainted with ship building, I do not expect you will be much assisted by him. I wish you had been mentioned at first on this business, that no time might have been lost; however, I make no doubt but that you will have your ship ready before some of those that are building to the northward. I shall be glad to have a line from you when any thing occurs, and am with compliments to your brother,

Dear sir, your most ob't humble serv't,

JOSEPH HEWES.

To Samuel Purviance, Jr. Esq., Baltimore.

No. 50.

In Committee of Safety,
New York, Feb'y 4, 1776.

Gentlemen,—We think it our duty to inform the continental congress, through you, that General Clinton of the ministerial troops, and one transport are this day arrived here, but we do not know that she contains any troops. That the Mercury ship of war is near Staten Island, coming into port.

We are well informed that those vessels left Boston not more than fourteen days ago.

The Mayor has this evening declared to us, that he was then come from Governor Tryon, and is authorised by the Governor to assure the inhabitants that no troops are coming here; that General Clinton was present, and said that no troops are coming here. That Governor Tryon further told that General Clinton had only called to pay him a short visit—that if any transport with troops should by accident or stress of weather put in here, they are not intended to remain here.

We do not rely on this information, but if it be true, we conceive that the most natural conclusion is, that he is going to the southward.

Major General Lee is arrived here this day, ill with the gout, and has sent over for Lord Sterling's regiment.

We are most respectfully, gentlemen, &c.

By order,

Jos. Hall, *Chairman*,

of the Committee of Safety of New York.

To the New York Delegates in Congress.

The above letter was sent by Mr. Chase from congress, to the Baltimore committee of correspondence.

No. 51.

Otter Sloop, Chesapeake Bay, March 8, 1776.

Sir,—I have just now received yours of this date, and have by Mr. Eddis, sent some pamphlets I received for you. My intention on my return was to have called at Annapolis, and sent them on shore by a flag of truce, as well as to purchase fresh provisions. I am sorry to find by your letter that the people of Annapolis should be under any apprehensions from their town being burnt or beat down. I must beg leave to assure you nothing of that kind will happen from me. I am on a cruize here in order to procure fresh provisions for the king's ships, and whenever I can be supplied with it, shall most readily pay the market price. I expect being at Annapolis in a few days.

I have the honor to be, sir,

Your most ob't humble serv't,

M. Squire.

To his Excellency Robert Eden, Esq., Governor of Maryland.

No. 52.

York Town, March 10, 1776.

Gentlemen,—This moment we received Mr. Alexander Donaldson's letter of the 9th inst. At the time of writing our former letter to him it was uncertain, from the intelligence, what force might be sent against Baltimore, and judged it would be proper for this county to have in readiness detachments from the several militia battalions, to the amount of five hundred men.

We are glad to hear that it is only the buccaneer Squire that payed you a visit, of whom we hope to hear Capt. Nicholson will give a good account. But as a greater force may be sent to harass you in revenge for

Capt. Squire's bad success ; in pursuance of the desire of your committee, communicated to us by Mr. Donaldson, our committee resolved instantly to raise a good rifle company, to be ready to march on an hour's warning to your province, in case you should judge it necessary, and signify the same to our committee.

The officers chosen are, Joseph Donaldson, captain ; William Rankin, first Lieutenant; John Kean, second Lieutenant ; Wm. Baillie, third Lieutenant, and Jacob Hottzinger, fourth Lieutenant ; and none are to be admitted but expert riflemen.

By order of the committee,

JAS. SMITH, *Chairman.*

To the Committee of Inspection, Baltimore.

No. 53.

Baltimore, March 12, 1776.

Gentlemen,—We have just now received your acceptable favor of the 10th, per Mr. Donaldson, and return you our warmest thanks for your ready offers of succour in defending us from the incursions of Captain Squire, who after taking many prizes at the mouth of our river, was obliged to relinquish the most valuable on the appearance of the gallant Capt. Nicholson, of the ship Defence, who has first had the honor of displaying the continental colors to a British man of war without a return.

The county of York have always stood in the foremost rank for zeal and attachment in the glorious cause of liberty, and this committee would do them an injury in refusing the rifle company to march at the first notice; they cheerfully then accept the generous offer, and will on any appearance of danger, inform them by express.

By order of the committee,

WM. LUX, *Dp. Chairman.*

To the Committee of York.

No. 54.

Frederick Town, March 10, 1776.

Gentlemen,—From advices received, we are apprehensive that before this time you must have had an attack from the ships of war belonging to the ministerial troops; our anxiety and feelings for the sufferings of our distressed brethren are almost beyond expression; we have, therefore, despatched an express to know whether you would wish the assistance of a battalion from the middle district of this county. If you should, and will procure an order for one from the council of safety, we are of opinion that out of the three battalions which we have the honor to command, one might be soon exceedingly well equipped with good arms, (bayonets excepted) fit for the field. We hope to have a full state of your situation by the return of the express, which we expect as soon as possible.

We are gentlemen, with great regard,

Your sincere friends,

C. BEATTY,

JAS. JOHNSON,

B. JOHNSON.

To the Committee of Correspondence for Baltimore town.

No. 55.

Baltimore, March 12, 1776.

Sirs,—The committee of Baltimore county beg leave to return you and the officers and men of your battalion, their thanks, for the alacrity shewn in marching down to the assistance of Baltimore town, on the late alarming attempt of Capt. Squire in the Otter sloop of war. It is owing to you, sirs, with your worthy officers and battalion, together with the other gentlemen of the militia, and the gallant Capt. Nicholson, with his officers and men, that we are preserved from the threatened danger, and knowing your attachment to the noble cause of liberty, we shall with confidence rely on your succour when any further hostile attempts are made.

I am, sir, your most ob't servant,
Per order of the committee,
WILLIAM LUX, *Dp. Chairman.*

To Cols. Hall and Rumsey, Harford county.

No. 56.

Antietem Furnace, 10*th March,* 1776.

Sir,—Mr. B. Johnson enclosed me your letter to Mr. Beatty and himself. It gives me very great concern to hear of your being in so much danger in Baltimore, and my not having it in my power to send so many guns as I expected. I have sent one yesterday, and three go to-day, which have stood the proof of 7¼ lbs. powder, two balls and two wads at first, and 6 lbs. powder, two balls and two wads the second time. I am convinced, they will do for service, and as you are so much in want of these, I have thought it best to send them down without being passed by the proper person. I shall continue to send as many as will stand this proof, and as fast as we can finish them. The powder we have used, is several degrees stronger than cannon powder; this will hereafter be considered. The miscarriage of the first proof put us at least a week back in our business, but we have recovered our spirits, and are determined to push with redoubled vigor. Should you refuse to take the guns I send down, I shall expect an express; otherwise, shall send all I can.

I am, your very humble servant,

S. HUGHES.

To Samuel Purviance, Baltimore.

No. 57.

Philadelphia, February 27th, 1776.

Gentlemen,—We take the earliest opportunity to send you the enclosed resolution of congress, and to request your immediate attention thereto, and that you will inform us of the number and circumstances of the permits which have been granted, and the destination of the vessels for exporting the produce of the colonies, in consequence of the importation of ammunition and warlike stores. We are appointed to make enquiry into this subject.

We are, gentlemen,

Your obedient servants,

—— DUANE, —— LIVINGSTON,
SAMUEL CHASE, GEORGE WYTHE.
JAMES WILSON,

To the Committee of observation for Baltimore town.

No. 58.

Philadelphia, 27th May, 1776.

Dear Sir,—I received your account of the re-taking Hudson's ship, and the flight of the enemy with great pleasure. I hope you will make wise use of the opportunity to render the avenues to your flourishing town, inaccessible to the enemy. I think you have the means of doing this most effectually, and sure it ought not to be neglected. I suppose the Defence and her tender, will now be employed in keeping your bay coast, as far as Potomac, clear of sloops and tenders from our enemies. I am sure Capt. Squires will not interrupt your trade, so long as he knows Capt. Nicholson is with you; and as for larger ships, if they should come, which is not very probable, it will be no difficult matter to get out of their way, by retiring to shallow water. I expect this will be delivered you by General Lee, who is on his way to his southern command. I am in no doubt of the worthy general meeting with those civilities from you, that prove so agreeable to every body else. It is of great importance that General Lee should quickly get to the place of his destination, and therefore, if he should want either horses or guides for this purpose, I know your patriotic committee will furnish them. I need not trouble you with news, as the general can give you any that prevails here.

I am, with much esteem, sir,

Your obliged and obedient servant,

RICHARD HENRY LEE.

To Samuel Purviance, Jr., Esq., Chairman of the Committee of Baltimore, favored by General Lee.

No. 59.

Joppa, April 6th, 1776.

Sir,—I have communicated your letter to the eighth battalion, who are much pleased that their conduct on the late alarm, occasioned by the Otter, has met with the approbation of so truly respectable a body as the committee of Baltimore county.

That battalion, sir, esteem it but their duty to march to the assistance of any part of this province when attacked, or in danger of it. But they march with greater alacrity to your assistance, from the pleasing memory of former connexions, and a sense of the value and importance of Baltimore town to the province in general.

You may, from the known and firm attachment of the battalion to the cause of liberty, rest assured that you will most certainly receive their succour, to repel all hostile attempts on it.

I am, sir,

Your most humble servant,

BENJAMIN RUMSEY.

Mr. Wm Lux, deputy chairman of the Committee of Baltimore county.

No. 60.

In Committee, Baltimore, 14*th, April,* 1776, 10 *o'clock, P. M.*

Honorable Sir,

The enclosed copies of letters were just now received by our committee, by express from the council of safety of Virginia, with desire that they might be forwarded to you instantly. Indeed, they contain matter, we think, of too much importance, to have been delayed a moment. In consequence whereof, we have prevailed on our commanding officer here, to appoint Mr. David Plunket, a lieutenant, in whose prudence and industry we can rely, to wait on you with this ; and if your honorable body should think it necessary to take any steps, or give any instruction to the council of safety on the occasion, he will wait your commands.

We have the honor to be,

With the greatest respect, honorable sir,

Your most obedient servants,

SAMUEL PURVIANCE, Jr., *Chairman*,

WM. LUX, *Vice Chairman*, JOHN SMITH,

JAMES CALHOUN, WM. BUCHANAN,

THOMAS HARRISON, JOHN BOYD,

BENJ. NICHOLSON, JOHN STERETT.

The honorable John Hancock, Esq., president of the congress, Philadelphia.

No. 61.

Philadelphia, April 16*th*, 1776.

Gentlemen,—I received, and immediately communicated to congress, your letter of the 14th, with the important papers enclosed. In consequence of which the congress have resolved, that the person and papers of Governor Eden be immediately seized by the committee of safety, to whom I write by this opportunity. The person mentioned in the enclosed resolution, (Mr. Alexander Ross,) is represented as a dangerous partizan of administration, who has lately been with Lord

Dunmore, and it is suggested, is on his way to the Indian country, to execute the execrable designs of our enemies. I have no doubt, but you will exert your utmost endeavors in seizing and securing him.

I am, with respect, gentlemen,

Your most obedient servant,

JOHN HANCOCK, *President.*

You will please not to make public mention of the resolution respecting Governor Eden, until the committee of safety have executed it.

To the honorable Committee of Baltimore.

No. 62.

Baltimore, 17*th April*, 1776.

Gentlemen,—We herewith transmit you copies of the resolve of congress, respecting the seizing and securing Alexander Ross, and the letter of the president of the congress, informing us of their resolution, that the person and papers of Governor Eden be immediately seized by our council of safety, to whom that resolution is transmitted. Instantly upon receiving your letter by express, we appointed three of our body to wait on the council of safety, to communicate the intelligence received, and to use their utmost endeavors to have Governor Eden put under arrest. Our council have thought it sufficient to take Governor Eden's parole of honor, not to depart the province, till the meeting of the convention of Maryland, and to promote the peace in the meantime, but we make no doubt that they will, upon receiving the resolve of congress immediately seize the person and papers of Governor Eden. We hope you will excuse our detaining your express.

I am, on behalf of the Committee,

Gentlemen,

Your most humble servant,

SAMUEL PURVIANCE, Jr. *Chairman.*

To the honorable Council of Safety of Virginia, Williamsburg.

No. 63.

Philadelphia, 1*st May,* 1776.

Dear Sir,—I thank you for your favor of the 23d April, which I should have answered before now, if I had not been prevented by much business. If zeal in a good cause may not cover small irregularities, or deviations from the strict line of office, and regard for the public safety be chained to the letter of business, I fear such pedantic politics will ruin America, as they must fatally injure every country where they prevailed. The public of America is a generous public, and when appealed to will readily distinguish things dictated by the general good, though irregularly executed, from such as are evil in their nature, and merely the suggestions of folly and wickedness. I am sure, a generous community will not suffer any person to be persecuted for the former, nor would I scruple in such a case, to say as of old, Provoco ad populum, and then look the proudest connexions in the face, trusting to the wisdom of the object, and the integrity of design, notwithstanding the manner might be something unusual.

I find Capt. Nicholson's merit is well understood here, and therefore I hope he will succeed in his desires.

I am, truly, your friend and obliged humble servant,

RICHARD HENRY LEE.

To Samuel Purviance, Jr., Esq., Baltimore, Maryland.

No. 64.

Philadelphia, May 6th, 1776.

Dear Sir.—I received yesterday, your favor of the 2d inst., and in answer to that part of it, desiring to know if Mr. Hancock gave a copy of your letter to any person, I must say that I do not know whether or not, but I am inclined to think he has not. This business appears to me thus :—when Mr. Hancock received the despatches from Baltimore, he proceeded to read the whole in congress; and among others, a letter containing observations on the council of safety of Maryland, relative to the timidity of their councils, which it appears he had not previously read in private ; because when he came to that part of it which mentioned its being written in confidence, he stopt, and observed it was private, and proposed it should be so considered ; but as he read so much of it, he went on, but read no name at the bottom; and in the debate consequent upon it, it was supposed to be anonymous, and it was conjecture alone that fixed you as the author. I should have certainly informed you of this, if I had then found myself at liberty to do it ; and when I heard from you of your summons before the convention, it was too late for a letter to reach you, before your appearance at that board. But the idea of drawing from the mouth of a person accused his own condemnation, is reprobated by English jurisprudence, and is the practice only, of inquisitorial or star chamber tyranny. I should incline to think that this persecution will be carried no further, at least I am sure the time is quickly coming, when violence from without will render absolutely necessary, a perfect union within. A late arrival from Port L'Orient, with 13 tons of powder and 30 of saltpetre, brings us a Cork paper near the middle of March, by which we learn that more than 40,000 men would sail from Portsmouth and Greenock about the 1st April, for North America. They consist of Hessians, Hanoverians, Mecklenburghers, Scotch Hollanders and Scotch Highlanders, with some British regiments. Their destination not certain, but said to be New York, New England, Canada, and two expeditions more south.

Should the persecutors go on against you, I would advise answering no interrogatories, but plainly detail my conduct, acknowledge such parts as were without the strict line of duty, and lay it to the account of my zeal for the cause of America, which I hoped a generous community would pardon and forget.

My time and attention are so taken up with public business, that I must now conclude, with referring you to my letter by Dr. Bankhead.

I am, with regard, dear sir,

Your friend and obedient servant,

RICHARD HENRY LEE.

To Samuel Purviance, Jr., Esq., of Baltimore, in Maryland.

No. 65.

Philadelphia, 2d June, 1776.

Sir,—I have received your favors of the 24th and 28th ult.; with respect to the former, I wish you could collect all the accounts that are yet unpaid for the two vessels fitted out by you and Mr. Lux, and settle them in such manner, that the marine committee may have nothing further to do with them than to order payment. As the men belonging to the Hornet and Wasp, at the time of their arrival here, have been discharged at their own request, being at that time very sick, some few of them may have entered again on board of some of the vessels, for ought I know; however, you are requested by the marine committee, not to advance any thing for any of them. I received your last letter to that board, who directed me to inform you, that cannon had been contracted for in this colony, for all the frigates, but as there is no certainty of getting them in any reasonable time, they wish you to get them for the frigate you are building. If I can get the dimensions of them to send by this post, you shall have them enclosed, if not I will send them by the next. I suppose it will be more convenient for you to get the cannon from Mr. Hughes' works, than from any other place. The committee intend to have all the frigates fitted out as fast as possible, and desire your board to furnish every thing for the one under your care. Your precaution in keeping a guard, I think a good one.

I am, with much respect, sir,

Your most obedient servant,

JOSEPH HEWES.

To Samuel Purviance, Jr., Esq., Baltimore.

No. 66.

Philadelphia, 2d July, 1776.

Dear sir,—When I wrote to you last, I believe I mentioned to you only two lieutenants for the ship. It was a mistake. Three are allowed to each of the frigates, so that, when Capt. Nicholson sends up a recommendation for sea officers, he should put down three lieutenants. Part of General Howe's army is arrived at Sandy Hook. We must expect warm work in that quarter in a few days.

I am, with respect, sir,

Your most obedient servant,

JOSEPH HEWES.

To Samuel Purviance, Jr., Esq., Baltimore.

No. 67.

Philadelphia July 4th, 1776.

Gentlemen,—The congress have this day received intelligence, which renders it absolutely necessary that the greatest exertion should be made to save our country from being desolated by the hands of tyranny. General Howe having taken possession of Staten Island, and the Jerseys being drained of their militia, for the defence of New York, I am directed by congress, to request you will proceed immediately to embody your militia for the establishment of the flying camp, and march them with all possible expedition, either by battalion, detachments of battalions, or by companies, to the city of Philadelphia.

The present campaign, I have no doubt, if we exert ourselves properly, will secure the enjoyment of our liberties for ever. All accounts agree, that Great Britain will make the greatest effort this summer. Should we, therefore, be able to keep our ground, we shall afterwards have little to apprehend from her. I do, therefore, most ardently beseech and require you, in the name and by the authority of congress, as you regard your own freedom, and as you stand engaged by the most solemn ties of honor, to support the common cause:—to strain every nerve to send forward your militia. This is a step of such infinite moment, that in all probability, your speedy compliance will prove the salvation of your country. It is impossible we can have any higher motive to induce us to act. We should reflect, too, that the loss of the campaign, must inevitably protract the war; and that in order to gain it, we have only to exert ourselves, and to make use of the means which God and nature have given us to defend ourselves. I must therefore again repeat to you, that the congress most anxiously expect and request, you will not lose a moment in carrying into effect this requisition, with all the zeal, spirit and despatch, which are so indispensably required by the critical situation of our affairs.

I have the honor to be, gentlemen,

Your most obedient and very humble servant,

JOHN HANCOCK, *President.*

Honorable Convention of Maryland.

No. 68.

Philadelphia, July 8th, 1776.

Gentlemen,—Although it is not possible to foresee the consequences of human actions, yet it is nevertheless a duty we owe ourselves and posterity, in all our public counsels, to decide in the best manner we are able, and to trust the event to that Being, who controls both causes and events so as to bring about his own determination. Impressed with this sentiment, and at the same time fully convinced that our affairs may take a more favorable turn, the congress have judged it necessary to dissolve all connexion between Great Britain and the American colonies, and to declare them free and independent states, as you will perceive by the enclosed declaration, which I am directed by congress to transmit to you, and to request you will have it proclaimed in your colony in the way you shall think most proper.

The important consequences to the American states from this declaration of independence, considered as the ground and foundation of a future government, will naturally suggest the propriety of proclaiming it in such a manner as that the people may be universally inform ed of it.

I have the honor to be, gentlemen,

Your most ob't humble servant,

JOHN HANCOCK, *President.*

Honorable Convention of Maryland.

No. 69.

Philadelphia, 25th June, 1776.

Sir,—Your favor of the 25th I laid before the marine committee last evening, and in answer thereto I have now to inform you, that when congress appointed the captains for the frigates, it was agreed that the rank should be settled hereafter, and that the captains should only at present be certified of their appointment. Captain Nicholson has been strongly recommended, and congress has a high opinion of his abilities and merit, and I have no doubt of his standing pretty high in rank. The marine committee will pay great attention to the recommendations of Capt. Nicholson, and your board of commissioners for building the frigates; but when you recommend two gentlemen for sea lieutenants, it would be well to get such of your delegates as may be in your province to join in such recommendation. I believe it will be agreeable to the committee that Capt. Nicholson should recommend all the warrant officers; in this, however, you can also join, and the committee will immediately transmit the warrants, filled up agreeably to such recommendation. The marine officers for your ship will be appointed to-day; their names you have below; the sooner Capt. Nicholson engages all the warrant and petty officers, the more agreeable it will be to the committee, who wish to have the ships ready soon as possible. I fear many of them will wait for guns and anchors.

I am, in haste, sir,

Your most ob't humble serv't,

JOSEPH HEWES.

John Stewart, Captain,
Thos. Pownal, 1st Lieut. } Marines.
Rich'd Harrison, 2d do.

N. B. Those gentlemen were strongly recommended by the delegates of your province, and I hope they will be agreeable to all.

To Samuel Purviance, Jr. Esq., Baltimore.

No. 70.

Philadelphia, 23d July, 1776.

Dear Sir,—I received your favor per Mr. Hughes, and immediately went with him to a member of committee for the cannon contracts ; they have agreed with him for a large quantity of cannon. My ill state of health has prevented me from attending much to business lately, and has obliged me for some time past to make an excursion or two into the country. I propose to return to North Carolina shortly, when I mean to retire from public business for a month or two. I have laid your accounts before the marine committee, and shall see that they are properly settled. I have not seen the person in whose favor you drew, and your brother is not in town ; to whom must the money be paid? I do not hear of any person that has been recommended as lieutenant for the ship you are building, nor have I as yet received your recommendations. Please to send me the names of these gentlemen in the order that you and Capt. Nicholson would wish them to stand ; I have mentioned Dr. Budd to the committee, he is not yet appointed ; I have no doubt but he will be, at the same time the lieutenants are appointed.

I am, with much respect, dear sir,

Your most ob't humble serv't,

Joseph Hewes.

To Samuel Purviance, Jr. Esq., Baltimore.

No. 71.

Philadelphia, 22*d* *July*, 1776.

Sir,—I have contracted with congress for 1000 tons of cannon, at £36 10*s*. to be delivered again the first January, 1778. I have had but little conversation with the marine committee about the frigate's guns; they seem to leave it to you and Capt. Nicholson to direct the length, 3 inches in or over; therefore hope you will send me the draft and direction, as soon as you can to the furnace, where I hope to be in 3 or 4 days. No news from New York. The militia of this province are marching daily to New York. The news of Clinton's defeat has raised their spirits in this place wonderfully.

I am, with regard,

Your very humble servant,

S. Hughes.

To Samuel Purviance, Esq., Baltimore.

No. 72.

Philadelphia, 16*th* *Sept.* 1776.

Dear Sir,—Since your brother left this city Mr. Nicholson has been confirmed first lieutenant of the Washington; and his worthy brother may be assured that in settling the ranks of the captains, his merit will not be forgotten. It is not probable that the frigates will sail in fleets for some time; and therefore it is likely that no higher appointment than that of captain will soon take place. It will be highly proper for Captain Nicholson to hasten on the Virginia (for that is most certainly the name of the Baltimore frigate) as much as possible. Her great obstruction, I fear, will be the anchors; however, we hope that will be removed ere long, as means have been taken to forward them.

You will shortly see published, the conference of our members with Lord Howe on Staten Island, in which you will find that his Lordship's much talked of powers are no more than to *confer* and *converse* with gentlemen of influence, and to prosecute the war! We anxiously expect here the issue of a long canonade at York, and another lately on Lake Champlain.

I am, sir, your most humble serv't,

RICHARD HENRY LEE.

To Samuel Purviance, Jr. Esq., Baltimore.

No. 73.

Philadelphia, 17*th Sept.* 1776.

Dear Sir,—Agreeable to my promise to your brother I now send a printed article for seamen. You will observe the wages allowed to able seamen is eight dollars per month; ordinary seamen and landsmen six dollars and two-thirds of a dollar per month.

I am, respectfully, dear sir,

Your most ob't servant,

JOSEPH HEWES.

To Samuel Purviance, Esq.

No. 74.

Philadelphia, 11*th October*, 1776.

Dear Sir,—Among the inconveniences of this busy scene, I esteem it not the least to be so often prevented from acknowledging the favors of my friends sooner than I do. It has been owing to much business that your letter of the 27th has not received an answer before now. I have the pleasure to acquaint you that in ranking the captains of our continental ships, the congress have placed Capt. Nicholson at the head, he being the first captain. I wish it were in my power to give you a satisfactory answer about the building another frigate. Hitherto nothing has been determined on this subject, the committee having been prevented by an infinite multiplicity of other business; and to the same cause has it been owing that no orders have been sent concerning the frigate Virginia. I have no doubt but that another frigate will soon be directed, and that the builder of greatest merit will be preferred. It would give me the greatest pleasure to hear that the Virginia was ready for sea, and I am happy in being satisfied that the managers of this business in Baltimore will not lose a moment in effecting so salutary a work. I suppose a want of anchors will be the greatest obstruction, as I take it for granted no time will be lost in getting the guns down from Mr. Hughes's works, and having the carriages made. I shall be glad to have an exact state of the frigate, and what she wants to complete her. I refer you to the papers for news, and am, sir,

Your most ob't servant,

RICHARD HENRY LEE.

To Samuel Purviance, Jr. Esq., Baltimore.

19

No. 75.

Philadelphia, 24th Nov., 1776.

Dear Sir,—You have imputed to the right cause my not answering your former letter sooner: it was indeed multiplicity of business.

Very long before your recommendation of Mr. Plunket came to hand, a Capt. Disney had been appointed captain of marines on board the Virginia, upon the recommendation of Mr. Stone. The congress have determined to build in Maryland two frigates of 36 guns each, and I make no doubt but that one at least of these will be built at Baltimore. I suppose when the committee meets on Tuesday next, that directions concerning the building the new ships will issue to the respective states. Not a word has been yet said in congress touching a quarrel with Portugal, nor will any such thing happen, I imagine, unless they should confiscate any of our vessels.

It will give us much pleasure to learn that Captain Nicholson is ready for sea, and I think we can furnish him from hence with one such anchor as you mention. Capt. Biddle's frigate Randolph, of 32 guns, is now completely ready, except that she wants men, which want we hope to remedy when the vessels, daily expected, arrive. The Virginia and the Randolph, cruizing together, might bring us in some of the enemy's scattering frigates that now go about, very badly manned, injuring our trade extremely. I wish, therefore, that every effort were strained to get the Virginia ready. Our enemy's army has been pretty busy since they retreated from the White Plains. Already they have got possession both of Mount Washington and Fort Lee, and they talk, or the Tories talk for them, strongly of their aiming at this city. I fancy they will find some difficulty and not a little danger in the accomplishment of this part of their plan.

My compliments, if you please, to the reverend Mr. Allison and my other friends in Baltimore.

If the Tories do not mend their manners, be more modest, and less noisy, they will shortly be hauled over the coals in such a manner as will make the country too hot to hold them.

I am, sir, your most ob't humble servant,

RICHARD HENRY LEE

List of new ships to be immediately undertaken.

New Hampshire, 1 ship of 74 guns.
Massachusetts, 1 ship of 74 guns, and 1 of 36 guns.
Pennsylvania, 1 ship of 74 guns, and 1 of 18 guns.
Maryland, 2 ships of 36 guns each.
Virginia, 2 do. do. do.

To Samuel Purviance, Jr., Esq., Baltimore.

P. S. Nov. 25, 1776—I thank you for your favor of the 22d, with its enclosures, and will answer your letter by next post, not being able now to do it with proper effect. I know we want vessels, both on charter and to purchase, in Virginia and Maryland. But more of this hereafter. Gen'l Howe seems intent on this city.

R. H. LEE.

No. 76.

Philadelphia, Dec. 27th, 1776.

Dear Sir,—An hour's detainment of the tide gives me an opportunity of writing the particulars of yesterday's action at Trenton. Gen'l Washington, with about four thousand men, crossed on the Christmas night, and surrounded the town; the enemy was surprised, and collected confusedly; after a short resistance they grounded their arms and surrendered to the amount of 750 (Hessians solely); they lost 30 killed and wounded, and we 2 killed and 3 or 4 wounded; Capt. Washington among the last, who commanded the advanced party, but not mortally. Had the weather proved favorable, and the other three divisions got over, there would (I have no doubt) the whole of them shared the same fate with those. Their light horse scampered away on the first alarm, and all those on the outskirts of the town made their escape, about as many as were taken. There are 1 colonel, 2 majors, 4 captains, 7 lieutenants and 8 ensigns prisoners, with 6 field pieces, 2 standards and 1000 stand of arms, 20 drums; one colonel wounded and left on his parole in Trenton. Our people having returned on this side again; we should have whipped them in the same manner at Bordentown, could our men under Col. Cadwallader have crossed, but the weather and ice made it impossible.—This affair has given such amazing spirit to our people, that you might do any thing, or go any where with them. We have vast numbers of fine militia coming in momently, but none from our province. I believe an attack is intended to-morrow upon the Hessian main body at Bordentown, in which I intend serving with my people as artillery men, and are embarked for that purpose on board the gallies. Immediately it is over (please God) I intend down, and am doubtful if I can bring an anchor with me, but more of this hereafter. (I am not pleased about it.)

I am yours, most sincerely,

JAMES NICHOLSON.

To Samuel Purviance, Jr. Esq., Baltimore.

No. 77.

Baltimore, 20*th Jan.* 1777.

Gentlemen,—Please to deliver Mr. Francis Lewis, a member of congress, one pair of blankets out of the continental stores, he to be accountable for the same.

RICHARD HENRY LEE,
FRAS. LEWIS,
WM. WHIPPLE.

To Messrs. Purviance.

No. 78.

Mr. Hancock's compliments to Mr. Purviance, and begs he would be kind enough to send him the price current he mentioned to him, and informs Mr. Purviance that it is the desire of the marine committee that he, with Mr. Stewart, would immediately give the necessary directions for cutting timber, and agreeing with persons for building the two frigates here. Mr. Hancock being much engaged in forwarding despatches, prevented his sending him the regular resolution, but he shall have them in the morning.

Tuesday Evening, Jan. 21, 1777.

No. 79.

Providence, Feb. 18th, 1777.

Sir,—The very great scarcity of flour, bread and iron in this state, and the danger of the inhabitants suffering for want of these necessary articles, have induced the council of war to fit out the sloop Diamond, Timothy Coffin, master, to your address to procure them.

We enclose you a draft upon the continental treasurer for a sufficient sum of money to lade her, and desire that you will put on board her ten tons of bar iron, if to be procured, otherwise fifteen tons of pig iron, to fill her hold with flour, and her steerage and cabin with as much bread as she can with any convenience take in.

I am, in behalf of the state, sir,

Your most ob't humble serv't,

NICHOLAS COOKE, *Governor.*

To Samuel Purviance, Esq.

No. 80.

Portsmouth, New England, Feb. 20, 1777.

Gentlemen,—I lately received an order from the honorable continental marine committee, to send two small vessels to Baltimore for iron and flour on account of the continent, to your address; in consequence of which I have sent the schooner Dove, Capt. James Miller, by whom this will be handed you, and by whom you will please ship as much iron and flour as the schooner will carry with safety, on account of the United States of America; as I am in much want of iron, you will please ship as large a proportion of that article as the vessel will bear. I shall want for the use of the continent at least forty tons of iron this season, the whole of which I hope will be sent, or more in this and the Friend's Adventure, which will sail in a few days for your place. Pray let about two and a half tons of iron be in very wide bars, suitable for making fire places on board ships; should also be glad of about two tons of nail rods assorted. Col. Whipple, who is one of the honorable committee, has wrote me from Baltimore that you would load and despatch the vessels on account of the continent.

I am, with all due respect, gentlemen,

Your most obedient servant,

JOHN LANGDON.

To Messrs. Samuel and Robert Purviance, Baltimore.

No. 81.

Philadelphia, 15*th April*, 1777.

Sirs,—I am favored with yours of the 12th inst. which I last night laid before the committee. In that letter you say you had transmitted to the *board*, inventories of the materials belonging to the ship and brigantines, but no such is come to hand, and Mr. Morris tells he has received none.

Such is the perplexed situation of our affairs at present, that nothing can be done relative to the ships, coals, &c., for yesterday the alarm guns were fired as a signal for nine ships of war coming up the bay, and General Howe's army is in motion, in order to attack this city, in a poor state for defence for the want of troops. Pray forward all you can from Baltimore, for without reinforcements the conquest of this city is inevitable. Therefore, it behooves you to turn out all the force you can, and speedily, or it will be too late.

I am, gentlemen,

Your very humble servant,

FRANCIS LEWIS.

To Messrs. Samuel and Robert Purviance, Baltimore.

No. 86.

Annapolis, April 17*th*, 1777.

Gentlemen,—I addressed the governor and council upon the subject matter of your favor, to take their direction, upon which they entertain some doubt; however, the governor is of opinion the pork ought to be charged to the continent; upon a supposition that the expedition into Somerset and Worcester counties was a measure concerted for the benefit of the states in general, as well as this in particular.

I am, very respectfully, gentlemen,

Your very obedient humble servant,

W. SMALLWOOD, *Brig'r General.*

To Messrs. Samuel and Robert Purviance, Baltimore.

No. 83.

Philadelphia, April 19th, 1777.

Gentlemen,—Your favors of the 12th and 15th inst., came duly to hand,—the first advising your purchase of flour and enclosing inventories of the two prize vessels. We think the flour was bought very reasonably, and mentioned it in congress, as proper to be delivered to the commissary at Baltimore, for the use of the army, which was agreed to, and he must settle with you for it. It would give us pleasure to hear that the Virginia, Capt. Nicholson was sailed, and your bay clear of the enemy's ships: there are several of them at Cape Henlopen, where they have done much mischief.

We are, gentlemen,

Your obedient humble servant,

By order of the Secret Committee,

ROBERT MORRIS, *Chairman.*

To Messrs. Samuel and Robert Purviance, Baltimore.

No. 84.

Philadelphia, June 10th, 1777.

Gentlemen,—The secrect committee are now preparing their accounts and papers, in order to report the state of them and their proceedings to congress ; and for this purpose, they must call on every body with whom they have transacted business, to render in their accounts speedily as possible. You will therefore be pleased to send us account sales of the goods put into your hands ; account of the purchases you made by order of this committee, and account current, the sooner the better.

I am, sirs,

Your obedient humble servant,

By order of the Committee,

Robert Morris, *Chairman.*

To Messrs. Samuel and Robert Purviance, Baltimore.

No. 85.

York, the 17*th November,* 1777.

* * * * * *

Dear Sir,—The affair of the Spanish fleet that you mention, we had heard of some time ago, and at the same time, that since the death of the king of Portugal, all differences were made up between the two courts, and orders were sent to South America to restore all things there to quiet. We hear nothing from Philadelphia, except that the inhabitants are in great distress for provisions. Both armies are still, and both have lately received reinforcements. A considerable part of General Gates's army will shortly join General Washington.

I am, dear sir,

Your most obedient and very humble servant,

Richard Henry Lee,

To Samuel Purviance, Jr., Esq., Baltimore.

No. 86.

York Town, January 12*th,* 1778.

Gentlemen,—I had the honor of receiving and reporting your letter of the 10th, to congress this morning. It is referred to the marine committee, from whence you will receive a proper reply, I hope by return of the post.

Congress having received information, by divers means, of the arrival of the cargo of salt, intimated in your letter above mentioned, framed the inclosed act of the present date, for securing, if possible, the whole for the use of the army, for which it is wanted in the extremest degree. As some days may elapse before the governor and council can act, I am directed to transmit the copy enclosed as above mentioned to you, and to request you to exert your endeavors to prevent a sale or removal of the salt, until his excellency shall give directions, in consequence of the present recommendation and resolve. The term "secure," in the latter part of the resolve, you may be assured, comprehends the idea of purchasing, and I have so explained it to the governor.

It is expected that every friend to these states in your town, will give you all needful assistance to serve the public in this momentous business; without salt, it will be impossible to lay up magazines of provision for the army, and I need not predict what will be the consequence of deficiency.

I am, with great respect,

Gentlemen,

Your obedient humble servant,

HENRY LAURENS, *President of Congress.*

To Samuel and Robert Purviance, Esqrs., agents for the United States at Baltimore.

No. 87.

Commercial Committee, York,
January 15th, 1778.

Gentlemen,—We are informed that you are building a small vessel, that will be ready for launching in a few days. We should be glad to know whether you will sell her, and what you will ask for her as she is when launched. We would wish for a speedy answer, as we shall look out somewhere else for a suitable vessel for our purpose, if we should not purchase that you are building.

We do not doubt at all, gentlemen, but that you could make it convenient to take bills on the commissioners at Paris, but we have not heard that congress had any thought of drawing on them. We hope you will be able to get the draft on the loan office, paid in negotiable certificates, otherwise we do not know how we shall be able to pay the balance, which it seems will be due to you.

We are, gentlemen,
Your obedient servants,
FRANCIS LEWIS,
WILLIAM ELLERY,
JAMES FORBES.

To Messrs. Samuel and Robert Purviance, Baltimore.

No. 88.

York Town, 17th February, 1778.

Gentlemen,—The day before I left Baltimore, it was reported that a large French ship was on shore, on the coast near Chincoteague, and that they were taking part of the cargo out, in order to lighten her.

The agent from France arrived here yesterday, and informs us that a 50 gun ship, laden for the congress, may be about this time expected at the Capes from St. Domingo, and is anxious to know if that ship reported to be on shore, may not be the same, of which please to get the best information you can and inform me. Also, whether the Virginia has embraced the opportunities of these fair winds to put to sea, which I am very anxious to know.

I am, gentlemen,

Your very humble servant,

FRANCIS LEWIS, *Chairman*

of Commercial Committee.

To Messrs. Samuel and Robert Purviance, Baltimore.

No. 89.

War Office, York, March 16*th*, 1778.

Gentlemen,—The board have been duly favored with yours of the 14th inst. They are happy to find you have had the important business of procuring tents for our army, in as good a train as circumstances will admit. From our loss of Philadelphia, the workmen who came out are dispersed to places in which trade is open, and therefore none can be expected from this state, and every sail maker the quarter master general could properly procure, being at work on tents. You will please to keep as much tent cloth as you can have made up by the first of May, and send the rest on to be made up under the direction of the quarter master general.

I am your obedient servant,

RICHARD PETERS.

By order of the Board.

If you could, by any means, continue to get the whole made up at Baltimore, it would be doing much service; as the workmen are every where exceedingly scarce. As the enemy will endeavor to push out early, the tents should be, by all means, ready the first of May. We shall be much distressed for want of tents, as so many were lost last year, from the lateness of the campaign; therefore, do exert yourselves to have them made, but do not detain the cloth on a great uncertainty.

If the Virginia cannot get out, but should return, cannot some of her hands be procured to make tents?

By order,

R. PETERS.

To Messrs. Samuel and Robert Purviance, Baltimore.

No. 90.

Navy Board, Middle District,
Baltimore, 25th June, 1778,

Gentlemen,—As we are sensible it must take some considerable time to examine and adjust your accounts, which must be for large sums of long standing, we cannot, with any tolerable conveniency, continue the board here for that purpose, and therefore request you will, as soon as may be convenient, forward the same to us at Philadelphia.

We are, gentlemen,

Your very humble servants,

FRANCIS HOPKINSON,
W. SMITH,
JOHN WHARTON.

To Messrs. Purviance and Stewart, Baltimore.

No. 91.

In Council, Annapolis, 17th February, 1779.

Sir,—We hoped to have got the Conqueror off on Monday; she went off, however, yesterday morning, and expect she got up last night. We expect the Chester will be ready before the Conqueror can get down. We have recommended the Conqueror to Capt. Nicholson's care, as also the Dolphin, to have her masts fitted.

It is very agreeable to us, that Capt. Nicholson should command the Conqueror; the moderation he has shown is highly praiseworthy in him, and pleasing to us; we had no idea of either of our captains commanding Capt. Nicholson. The Commodore goes in the Chester, and from his disposition we expect the greatest harmony. We have no objection to putting in three lieutenants for this service.

We shall most cheerfully recommend any application for giving the whole of the prizes to the captors, nor doubt the success of it, so that we do not esteem it of any very great consequence, what they would be entitled to under the subsisting regulations, though we believe it is the same as in the continental service.

Bread, flour, meat, ammunition, and muskets, shall be all ready here to be put on board instantly. We are preparing for the Chester, and the like provision will be made for the Conqueror.

We shall be greatly at a loss for a surgeon, unless one can be got from Baltimore; it is desirable that one *good* one should go, and a mate. We have only one belonging to our marine, and we expect nothing further of him than to act as a mate.

Enclosed you have a line to Major Smith, to furnish what of the mattresses may be wanting, a lieutentant, sargeant, corporal, and not exceeding sixteen privates.

We are, sir,

Your most obedient servant,

THOMAS JOHNSON.

To Samuel Purviance, Jr., Esq., Baltimore.

No. 92.

To the Honorable Committee.

Gentlemen,—We, the officers on board the Conqueror Galley, beg leave to lay before their honorable body our petition. Should we have, in the time of the cruize, the bad fortune to be taken prisoners, will undoubtedly be confined on board some prison ship, and as we are protecting the trade of private property, should be glad to know if our wages will be continued, and by which way we may expect to be exchanged, as the greatest part are married men, and by long confinement our families would suffer. Therefore, we hope their honorable body will take into consideration our grievances. But should we receive no address, it shall not in the least detain our services from the cause in which we are now engaged. We have nothing more to add, but beg leave to subscribe ourselves,

Gentlemen,

Your most obedient humble servants,

JAMES NICHOLSON, JEREMIAH HUDSON, *Master*,
THOMAS MOORE, THOMAS DOYLE, *4th Lieut.*,
JOHN MARTIN, JOSEPH HARRISON, *Surgeon*.
ROBERT CAULFIELD,

March 4th, 1779.

No. 93.

Hampton Roads, April 3d, 1779.

Gentlemen,—It gives me no small concern to inform you that we have not, until these few days past, had it in our power to answer the purpose of our coming down, owing to the severity of the weather and the want of a pilot, the last of which we have now procured, after being detained three days in Cherrystone, where the severity of the weather forced us. We have been on the sea board for these two days past, and are now on our way convoying several merchantmen out, amongst which are Capts. Dill and Yellott. You may depend (I think) we shall defend the entrance and bordering of the bay from any cruizers inferior to frigates. Our galley answers our most sanguine expectations in point of sailing, &c., and I have to entreat, that should we not be fortunate within our two months, nor have it in our power to prevail with our people to continue one month extra, in that case, that you retain such sums as would fit us out for two months longer. We have lost one half of our time as above, and the season most favorable for the galleys will only take place by the time our cruize expires. We have not heard of any of the enemy being in the bay, since we have been down, nor do I believe there has been; but am very apprehensive they have made a great number of captures to the eastward, as we have heard of very few arrivals. We expect to be joined by the two Virginia ships to-morrow; they are no great things. I like their captains, who I think will do all in their power to assist us. I have not had it in my power to write you

20*

before. Our rendezvous is at Cape Charles or Isaac's shoals, where your outward bound vessels I would recommend should call. Should they not find us there, they may depend the coast is clear within our reach, and that we are extending our ground. They will also hear of us at Hampton, should they not be able to come to the Cape. At present our commodore does not seem extensively inclined, but I think after the Tender returns, if he will not go further to the northward or southward, if agreeable to my officers, we will go without him. For further particulars refer to Capt. Moore, who has got a memorandum of such articles as we are in want of, which I hope you will indulge us with, and send by the return of the Tender. The weather has been exceedingly bad. Good living has been all our comfort.

I am, gentlemen, with much respect,

Your most obedient servant,

JAMES NICHOLSON.

To the Honorable the Committee of Merchants of Baltimore.

No. 94.

In Council, Annapolis, 20th May, 1779.

Sir,—In yours of the 17th, you mention that salt provisions may be had in Baltimore for the Conqueror, on returning it or paying for it. We imagine that what was sent down in the boat and returned would serve for some time. It had best be so applied, and if more is wanted, that it had best be furnished out of that sent up in the Smallwood. The officers you mention in yours of yesterday are very agreeable to us. The Independence wants a good deal done to her to fit her for a cruize; the men we have are at present divided between her and the Chester: they in concert with our fort might be useful against vessels; the same end would be answered to you by the Baltimore and Johnson, they are gunned. We have them ready to send to Indian landing, with pork and other articles, but if you can get a force to use them as batteries, Baltimore town may have them for that purpose, if men can be engaged to carry up the Baltimore and Johnson, and act in them in case it should become necessary. We will on this occasion draw their pay for the little time they can be wanted out of the treasury, and risk the assembly's approbation of your conduct. The stores proposed by Capt. Nicholson appear reasonable to us. We wish you to lay in exactly the same for the Chester, except meat, which we can furnish them.

We are, sir,

Your most obedient servants,

THOS. JOHNSON.

To Samuel Purviance, Esq., Baltimore.

No. 95.

In Council, Annapolis, 28th July, 1780.

Gentlemen,—We have enclosed you the letter we have wrote to our delegates in congress on the subject of the distresses of our trade, for your perusal, which we request you to seal and send forward.

We are, gentlemen,

Your most ob't humble servants,

THOMAS S. LEE.

To Samuel and Robert Purviance, Esqrs. and others, merchants in Baltimore town.

In Council, Annapolis, 28*th July,* 1780.

Gentlemen,—The general assembly on the 12th June last, took into consideration the trade of this state, and entered into the following resolution:—"Resolved, that congress be informed that the trade of this state and Virginia, through the Capes of Chesapeake bay, is very considerable, and that this state and the United States are greatly interested in its preservation, and that this state has always contributed to the expenses of the continental navy, but the state or its trade has never received any benefit or advantage from the marine of the United States, and therefore that congress be earnestly requested to direct one of the continental frigates to be so stationed as to protect the trade from this state and Virginia, and further to order, (when the service of the United States will permit) that one of the frigates convoy the fleets from this bay,"—which was transmitted to congress, and by them referred to the board of admiralty, the result of whose deliberations thereon has not yet been communicated to us; nor do we know that the requisition of the assembly will be complied with. Our coast has lately been much infested with the privateers and cruizers of the enemy; our trade and navigation obstructed, and many of our vessels captured, to the great detriment of the public, and ruin of some and distress of many of our merchants; and we can assure you, unless two, or one at least of the continental frigates are so stationed as to afford protection to the trade of Virginia and this state, that there is little or no probability of our providing clothing and other necessaries for our quota of the army. As this state have on every occasion exerted themselves in an extraordinary degree in support of the common cause, and have and do contribute their proportion of the expense of the continental navy, and have not hitherto received any advantage from it; we can but think it reasonable that our request should be gratified. We have just received a letter from the commercial gentlemen of the town of Baltimore, representing that the successes of small armed vessels and boats have invited a very formidable enemy into our bay, and that not less than twenty of their most valuable vessels outward bound, are now blocked up in Patuxent river, and have been for some time past, and that every day they receive accounts of their vessels being taken or destroyed. This representation of the distresses and embarrassments of the trade and navigation of the states of Virginia and Maryland not only merit the immediate notice of congress, but we think cannot fail to induce them to order such a number of frigates to be stationed at the Capes of the Chesapeake as will afford ample protection to the commerce thereof. We entreat you in the most earnest manner to lay this important subject before congress, and to use your utmost efforts and the weight and influence of this state to obtain the protection desired.

We are, gentlemen,

With great respect and esteem,

Your most ob't humble servants,

THOMAS S. LEE.

To the Honorable the Delegates in Congress from Maryland.

No. 96.

Annapolis, Nov. 12th, 1780.

Gentlemen,—I am favored with your letter of the 10th, accompanied with the resolution and subscription of the merchants of Baltimore town. The public spirit and disinterestedness manifested by the measures which that respectable body have promptly taken, claim my full approbation, and I do not hesitate to assure you I have the utmost confidence in the disposition of the legislature to indemnify you fully in every of your measures, as well that of ordering an armed vessel to prevent any but vessels of a certain description from leaving the harbor whilst your preparations were carrying on, as the engagements you have made with the proprietors of the brig and schooner. The former I esteem very necessary and prudential, and which I have no doubt the council would have advised, had the propriety of it occurred in the hurry of writing you.

Mr. Purviance arrived here yesterday just after both branches of the legislature adjourned to Monday, or their answer might have been more satisfactory, and at my request he waited till this morning that I might have an opportunity of consulting the council, but I have not seen more than Mr. Carroll and Mr. Jno. Brice this morning, who approve of this letter. I have Col. Smith's by Capt. Revelley, and request you to assure him that the commissions desired shall be made out in time for the officers, and that the captain shall have every assistance in equipping the barge and men promised.

With sentiments of great respect and esteem,

I am, gentlemen,

Your most obedient servant,

THOMAS S. LEE.

To Samuel and Robert Purviance, Esqs. and others, merchants in Baltimore town.

No. 98.

Philadelphia, 27*th Feb.* 1781.

Dear Sir,—The Marquis La Fayette will pass by your city in a very short space with a very respectable detachment from General Washington. His movements will be as rapid as possible, therefore the supplies for his troops should be very certain; every thing in the provision way is sent from hence, except flour, and that might also be forwarded, provided shallops were to be had from hence, and teams to cart it from Christiana to Elk; it seems also like sending coals to New Castle, to send flour from hence to Baltimore; therefore, to ward against every chance of disappointment, we beg of you to procure and put into the care of Mr. Donnelan, commissary of issues at Baltimore, two hundred barrels of flour, or so much in addition to what he may have on hand, as to make up the quantity of two hundred barrels. We give you this trouble, because we do not know who is the superintendent of purchase for the state of Maryland, whose residence may also be out of the way of this express, and also to avoid every possible delay on this occasion. If Mr. Donnelan has flour on hand, or can instantly get it from the state agent, you will have no further trouble, but should neither be the case, and yourself and your brother merchants will please to furnish it, and be assured of having it replaced as speedily as possible out of the public magazine, of equal quality. We shall make no further apology at present for giving you this trouble, as we are assured of your readiness to do essential service to your country on every occasion. We shall write by next express more particularly, and are, dear sir,

Your most obedient servants,

TIM. PICKERING, Q. M. G.
CHAS. STEWART, C. E. S.

To Samuel Purviance, Esq., Baltimore.

No. 99.

In Council, Annapolis, 20th March, 1781.

Gentlemen,—We received your letter of the 10th, covering the engagement of the gentlemen of Baltimore, and an extract of a letter from Mr. McHenry of the 6th.

We very much applaud the zeal and activity of the gentlemen of Baltimore, and think their readiness to assist the executive, at a time when they were destitute of the means of providing those things which were immediately necessary for the detachment under the command of the Marquis de la Fayette, justly entitle them to the thanks of the public.

We cannot but approve of the proceedings of those gentlemen, and assure you we will adopt any expedient to prevent any individual of that body, from suffering, or being in the least embarrassed by his engagements for the state.

As soon as we are informed by the Committee of the amount of the sum advanced by their constituents, and the extent of their engagements, to procure the numerous articles required for the use of the detachment, we will transmit orders on the collectors of Baltimore county, for such a sum as will cover the whole.

We think it reasonable the state should pay the value of money advanced, and interest thereon until paid, and do agree to pay the value with interest, to those gentlemen who have made advances, and will give an order on the collectors of Baltimore for their reimbursement.

We are, gentlemen,

With very great respect and esteem,

Your most obedient humble servants,

THOMAS S. LEE.

To Robert Purviance, Matthew Ridley, and William Patterson, Esqrs., Baltimore.

No. 100.

In Council, Annapolis, 8th November, 1781.

Gentlemen,—The enclosure is a copy of a letter just received from the mouth of Patuxent, by which you will perceive, that some of the enemy's vessels are at present in that river. We hope there may be some vessels equipped in your harbor of sufficient force to prevent their getting off with their booty.

The value of the vessels and the great plunder they are probably encumbered with, make them an inviting object of profit, while their force is not so considerable as to discourage an attempt. Our state boats are down the bay, and may probably join any vessels you may send.

We can send 15 or 20 soldiers to assist in manning them, and will cheerfully render every assistance in our power, as to arms and ammunition.

We are, gentlemen, with respect,

Your most obedient servants,

THOMAS S. LEE.

To William Smith and Samuel and Robert Purviance, Esqrs., Baltimore town.

No. 101.

By the United States in Congress assembled, July 23d, 1781.

Resolved, That five suitable persons be appointed and authorized to open a subscription for a loan of thirty thousand dollars, for the support of such of the citizens of the states of South Carolina and Georgia as have been driven from their country and possessions by the enemy; the said states respectively, by their delegates in congress, pledging their faith for the repayment of the sums so lent with interest, in proportion to the sums which shall be received by their respective citizens, as soon as the legislatures of the said states shall severally be in condition to make provision for so doing, and congress hereby guarantee this obligation.

That the said five persons do also receive voluntary and free donations to be applied to the further relief of said sufferers.

Ordered, That the president send a copy of the above resolution to the executive of the several states, not in the power of the enemy, requesting them to promote the success of the said loan and donation, in such way as they shall think best.

July 24th, 1781.

Resolved, That Messrs. William Bingham, John Bayard, George Mead, Jacob Barge, and Doctor Hutchinson, be and they are hereby appointed and authorized to open a subscription for a loan, agreeable to the resolution, passed yesterday.

Extract from the minutes,

CHARLES THOMSON, *Secretary*.

www.ingramcontent.com/pod-product-compliance
Lightning Source LLC
LaVergne TN
LVHW050625100826
845148LV00011B/1733

* 9 7 8 0 7 8 8 4 5 1 3 2 4 *